The Complete Photo Guide to

DOLL MAKING

Creative Publishing international

Copyright © 2010 Creative Publishing international, Inc.
First published in the United States of America by
Creative Publishing international, Inc., a member of
Quayside Publishing Group
400 First Avenue North
Suite 300
Minneapolis, MN 55401
1-800-328-3895
www.creativepub.com

Printed in China
10 9 8 7 6 5 4 3 2 1

Library of Congress Cataloging-in-Publication Data

Hoerner, Nancy.
  The complete photo guide to doll making / Nancy Hoerner,
Barbara Matthiessen, Rick Petersen.
    p. cm.
  Summary: "Techniques and projects in step-by-step format for
making all kinds of dolls"–Provided by publisher.
  ISBN-13: 978-1-58923-504-5 (soft cover)
  ISBN-10: 1-58923-504-5 (soft cover)
  1. Dollmaking. 2. Dollmaking–Pictorial works. I. Matthies-
sen, Barbara. II. Petersen, Rick. III. Title.

  TT175.H627 2010
  745.592'21–dc22

2010000688

Visit www.Craftside.Typepad.com for a behind-the-scenes
peek at our crafty world!

Copy Editor: Cathy Broberg
Book Design: Kim Winscher
Page Layout: Linnea Fitzpatrick
Photographer: Corean Komarec
Photo Coordinator: Joanne Wawra

Acknowledgments

Thanks to my dear friend Elaine for helping me through some
very trying times. She has been a lovely gift. Also, I thank
my coauthors for their hard work. This book is what happens
when friends work together.
– Nancy

My gratitude to my husband Larry, for his patience and to my
grandchildren, Dylan, Riley, Lily, Freya and Ike, for inspiring
me to make safe toy dolls they enjoy.
– Barbara

Thank you to my wife, Margaret, for understanding my
need to be creative and giving me the space to do it; and to
my son, Benjamin, and daughter, Emily, for sharing my excite-
ment for art.
– Rick

The Complete Photo Guide to
DOLL MAKING

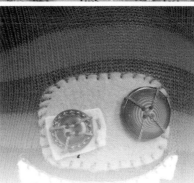
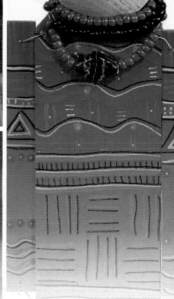

Creative Publishing
international

CONTENTS

Introduction	**6**
TOY DOLLS	**8**
SOCK DOLLS	10
Baby Doll	11
Santa Doll	14
Pillow Doll	22
Topsy Turvy Doll	26
Ballerina Doll	34
Woolen Baby Doll	38
Tara	48
NATURE DOLLS	**54**
Rock and Bark Faces	56
Sarah Jane Pin	58
Twig Doll	60
Corn Husk Doll	62
FOLK DOLLS	**64**
Spool Doll	66
Spoon Doll	70
Clothespin Doll	74
Yarn Doll	78
Hankie Dolls	82
Garden Glove Doll	86
PAPER DOLLS	**88**
Paper Faces	90
Painting Paper	94
Little Dolls That Move	98
Paper and Stick Doll	100
Tall Paper Doll	102
Punch, Judy, and Lulu Puppets	104
Paper Doll Chain	106

BOOK DOLLS 108
Techniques for Book Dolls 110
Sunny Day Journal 114
Flat Alice Travel Doll 116
Fabric Journal Doll 118

CLAY DOLLS 122
Armatures 124
How to Work with Clay 127
Sculpted Heads 128
Sculpted Hands and Feet 132
Tweaked Push Mold Faces 136
Garden Fairy 140

CLOTH ART DOLLS 152
Clay Faces and Hands 154
Art Doll with Clay Face I 156
Art Doll with Clay Face II 158
Cloth Dolls with Needle-
    Sculpted Faces 160
Cloth Doll with Encaustic Face 166

Art Doll Gallery 168
Embroidery Stitches 179
Patterns 182
Resources 206
About the Authors 206
Index 207

Introduction

Welcome to the wonderful world of dolls. In this book you will find techniques and step-by-step directions for making all kinds of dolls—toy dolls to multimedia art dolls and everything in between. The possibilities for doll making are nearly endless and each doll can become a small, personal work of art.

Dolls allow us to express ourselves in unique ways. Making dolls of fantasy creatures, iconic beauty, or pure whimsy lets us explore techniques, learn skills, and explore concepts. Creating dolls from unusual materials, natural materials, or found objects is exciting and expands your artistic vision.

The instructions in this book along with the step-by-step photographs will guide you through the various techniques and processes of doll making. You will be able to re-create the pictured dolls but are encouraged to add your own personality by using your favorite colors, embellishments, hair, and eye colors. Feel free to use the method for making hair from one doll with the face from another and construction technique from a third. By integrating a variety of techniques and by using your favorite materials and colors, you will have a personally meaningful creation.

Most of us recall a doll or two from our childhood, and if we are lucky, we might still have these treasures. There is an emotional connection to these dolls that we played with, hugged, dragged around, dressed and undressed thousands of times. When you make a doll for a child, you are supplying them with a playmate, something to snuggle with and treasure. Check out the toy doll chapter for a number of options sure to delight any child.

Folk and nature dolls are the wonderful dolls made from things around the yard and house—wooden spools that once held sewing thread, clothespins, a discarded wooden spoon, or twigs. Most of these dolls originated long ago when people used the materials they had on hand to create dolls. Add in some bits of yarn, a scrap of fabric, buttons, or stones to make one of these your own.

The paper dolls in this book are not the accordion fold-and-cut variety we all know and love but rather unique dolls made from paper. Using posterboard or heavier paper requires some creative treatments to make it work visually. Various types of collage are the answer. With your custom-made decorative paper, you can make a variety of imaginative paper dolls.

Journaling has become very popular, and with that popularity the desire to craft a personal journal has grown. You will learn to construct doll books and learn the pamphlet stitch, which is just one way of holding the pages and cover together into a book.

With the invention of polymer clays, doll making advanced to the point of near realism. You will learn the skills needed to work with polymer clay and special tools to create some incredible dolls. Making multimedia or mixed media dolls is a challenging adventure, but one that many doll makers find incredibly expressive and enjoyable. We show you some of our own mixed-media dolls along with some inspiring examples made from found objects.

Making a doll is like creating a little person with all of the wonders that includes. Anyone who has made dolls knows that at some time in the process the dolls develop a mind of their own. You first start noticing it when the dress you made just doesn't fit right and she gives you a sad look. Or you give her brown hair and it droops. She knows that she wants blond, bouncy hair and pink cowboy boots. When you finally find the key, the "aha moment," both of you are happy. That little spark, that something you can't describe, is what makes a doll a great doll. We hope you see this "aha" magic in the dolls that we have created for you and in the dolls you handcraft yourself.

TOY DOLLS

Making dolls for children is fun, economical, and a great way to create a treasured memory. Who does not remember a handmade doll? In this section you will find a number of types and styles of toy dolls to choose from. Create heart-warming memories and delight a child today with one of these dolls.

Toy Doll Safety

There are a number of safety factors to keep in mind when making dolls for children. For children under three, there must be no small parts that could fit into their mouths. Do not use buttons, snaps, beads, or any other embellishment or doll part that might cause choking. Dolls should be too large to fit all the way into a child's mouth. You can purchase tubes made to test safe sizes at larger toy stores. Embellish with embroidery or non-toxic no VOC paints.

Dolls for children ages three to six can have large buttons, beads, bells, or other embellishments; however, check with parents about the maturity of their child before adding these items. Safety eyes are approved for this age group but forgo button eyes unless parents approve.

For all children, make sure all materials used to create the doll are non-toxic; if in doubt, do not use it. Prewash all materials in approved laundry soap. Create sturdy dolls. It is better to make a long-lasting doll that can stand to be played with for years than an artistic one that will last an afternoon.

Sock Dolls

Sock dolls, these soft charmers, are a good introduction to doll making. They require easy-to-find, inexpensive materials, simple sewing, and no tedious shaping.

Perhaps the first sock doll you make is from materials, odd socks, and stuffing you have on hand. Children enjoy making simple sock dolls in the form of snakes or bugs while some teens and adults have fun making outrageous monster dolls. The range of possibilities and ease of construction make sock dolls very popular.

Supplies

When choosing socks, the most important consideration is the tightness of the knit. You want to make sure that when you stretch the sock you do not see large gaps between the fibers where stuffing will show through. Loose knits will also make embroidery difficult. How the sock feels against your skin is important, too, since most sock dolls are destined to be held and cuddled. Natural fibers like cotton have a nice hand to them and bamboo is becoming a favorite for its silky touch. Wash all socks

to make sure they are colorfast and preshrunk and to remove any sizing. You will usually need at least two socks to complete a doll.

Bamboo, polyester, or cotton batting will all work for the stuffing or filling. The fluffier the stuffing, the easier it will be to get a nice smooth shape.

Sock dolls can be sewn completely by hand with thread and needle or constructed using a sewing machine for the larger seams. You will need scissors, pins, needles, and thread. Yarns, fibers, torn fabric strips, sock pieces, paint, or markers are commonly used to create hair on sock dolls. Embroidery floss with embroidery needle, fabric markers, or paint supplies can be used for their faces. You may want to dress up your doll with ribbons, trims, buttons, beads, felt, or fabric scraps.

Diagrams/Patterns

Proportional diagrams are better suited than patterns when working with socks since socks vary greatly in size and degree of stretch. Heads are formed from the toe sections, bottoms from the heels, and limbs from the rest of the sock.

BABY DOLL

This is one of the simplest of all dolls and ideal for baby's first doll.

Please read about toy safety (page 9) before beginning.

YOU WILL NEED

- two flesh-tone anklet socks, child or baby size
- one colored anklet sock, child or baby size
- black or blue embroidery floss
- red or pink embroidery floss
- sewing thread to match flesh-tone and colored sock
- basic sewing supplies

(continued)

1 Cut the cuff off a flesh-tone sock. Turn the cuff and the other sock inside out. Sewing by hand or machine, sew through both layers of the separated cuff, dividing it into two arms, and leaving a narrow space between them. Leave the tops open and stitch the bottoms closed in a slight curve. On the cuff of the whole sock, stitch the legs in a similar way.

2 Carefully cut apart the arms and between the inner leg seams. Trim any excess fabric along the curves. Cut a small slit in the sock sole.

3 Turn the legs and body right side out through the small slit. Turn the arms right side out. Stuff the body, making the toe section round for the head. Stuff the legs and arms. Do not stuff tightly. Ladder stitch the opening closed.

4 Turn under the open end of each arm and pin the arms to the shoulders. Stitch the arms onto the body.

5 To form the feet, stitch a knot at the ankle with doubled thread. Wrap the thread tightly around the ankle two or three times. Take a small stitch over the thread wraps, knot, and trim off the thread. Repeat for the wrists and neck.

6 Embroider the face using your choice of floss colors. To mark the location of the eyes, place a pin horizontally across the center of the face and another vertically down the center. Thread an embroidery needle with six strands of eye-color floss. For dolls that will have hair or a hat, secure the floss at the top back of the head where it will be covered. Bring the needle down through the head, coming out just above and to the right of the center.

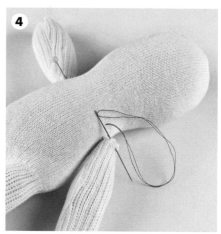

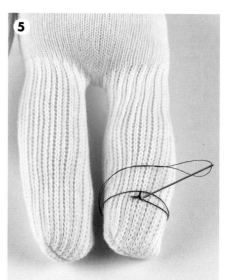

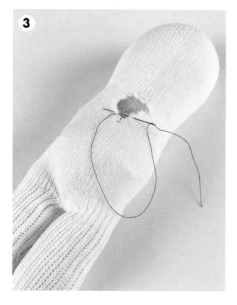

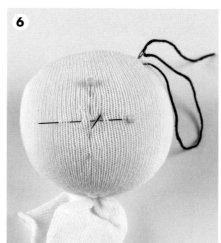

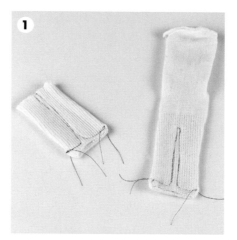

7 Stitch a French knot (page 181). Make sure to cross at least one knit stitch in the sock, so the eye will not pull back under the fabric.

8 Bring the needle all the way through to the top back of the head, and take a small stitch. Insert the needle back to the front of the face on the opposite side of the center, and stitch another French knot. Bring the needle to the back of the head and knot off.

9 Following the same method, use mouth-color floss to embroider a single straight stitch for the mouth, placing the stitch below and centered to the eyes.

10 Make a romper and hat from a colored sock. Cut off the cuff for a hat. Cut off and discard the heel, leaving the toe and foot. The toe will become the bottom of the romper. Flatten out the toe area, and mark the center ½" (1.3 cm) of the toe with two pins. Cut a ¼" (6 mm) slit on each side of the center pins, for inserting the legs. Cut ¼" (6 mm) arm holes at the sides, 1" (2.5 cm) down from the open end.

11 Slip the romper onto the doll with arms and legs going through the slits. Allow the top edge of the sock to curl down slightly. Slipstitch the romper top to the doll's neck.

12 Turn the cuff piece inside out. Gather the raw edge together by using a running stitch pulled tight; knot off the thread. Turn the hat right side out. Place the hat on the doll's head, covering the embroidery knots on the back. Slipstitch the lower edge of the hat to the doll's head.

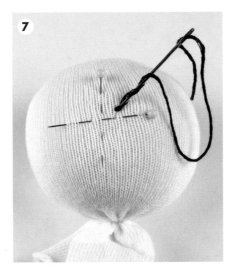

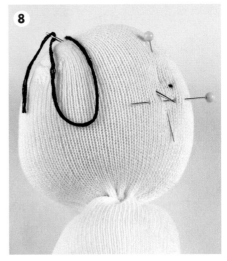

Tip

If you cut the arm or leg holes too large, slipstitch the holes together using matching thread.

SANTA DOLL

This doll is slightly more complex than Baby Doll, with a separate head, beard, and embellishments. This doll is designed for older children for whom button eyes and small embellishments are considered safe. To adapt this doll for younger children, just omit buttons and other embellishments and embroider the features instead.

YOU WILL NEED

- one flesh-tone bobby sock
- two red bobby socks
- white yarn
- two black shank buttons, ¼" (6 mm)
- metallic button, 1" (2.5 cm)
- jingle bell, ¾" (19 mm)
- black felt: 4" x 4" (10.2 x 10.2 cm) and 1" x 12" (2.5 x 30.5 cm)
- green felt: 4" x 5" (10.2 x 12.7 cm)
- red, black, and green embroidery floss
- stuffing
- threads to match socks and felts
- basic sewing supplies
- cardboard: 5" x 4" (12.7 x 10.2 cm)

1 Cut across one red sock in the center between the toe and heel to form the body and legs. (The trimmed-off toe area will be used for the hat later.) Cut the cuff off the second red sock for the arms. Cut across the center of the flesh-tone sock between the toe and heel for the head. Cut a 1" (2.5 cm) circle from the remaining flesh-tone sock.

2 Turn the red sock body/legs and arm sections inside out. Following the illustration, stitch two arms from the short cuff piece, leaving one end of each arm open and curving the other end to the side fold. Center the heel of the body/leg piece and stitch inner leg seam. On ends of legs, stitch in an arc to round off feet. Cut arms apart and carefully; cut open inner leg seam.

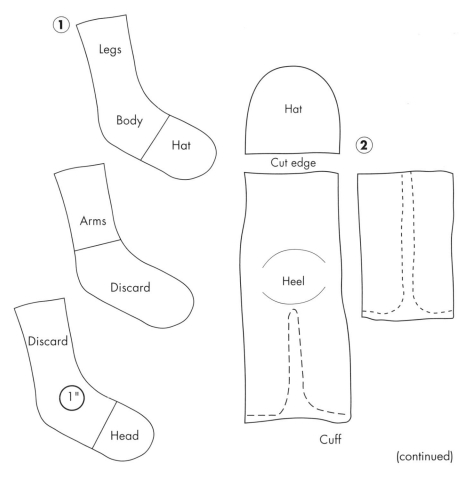

(continued)

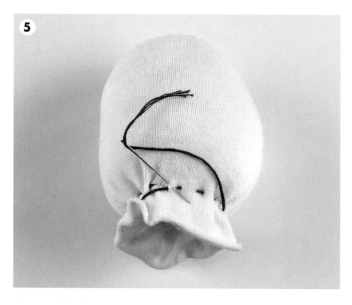

5

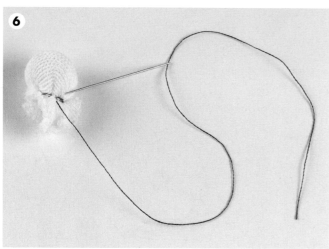

6

7 Stitch on button eyes using floss. Tie a double knot on end of the floss or stitch a knot on top of the head. Push needle down to one side of center for first eye, add button, and then insert needle a few threads over from where it exited. Push the needle back up to top of head, pulling button eye in slightly. Take a stitch. Repeat for second eye. Do not cut off floss.

8 Stitch a mouth ½" to ¾" (1.3 to 1.9 cm) below the eyes. Use a satin stitch to create a ½" x ¼" (1.3 cm x 6 mm) rectangle. Not much of the mouth will be seen. Push needle to back of the head. Take a stitch; then knot off.

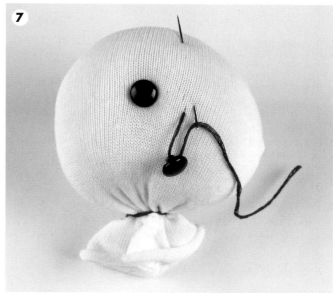

7

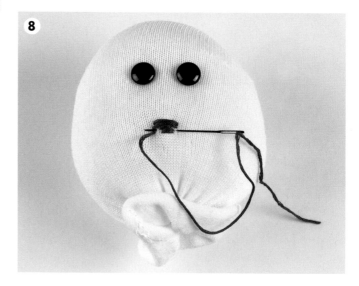

8

3 Turn the arms and body/legs right side out. Stuff both smoothly.

4 Stitch arms to the body 1½" (3.8 cm) from the top. (Refer to Baby Doll Step 4)

5 Gather bottom of trimmed flesh-tone sock using a running stitch, about 1" (2.5 cm) from the open edge. Stuff sock smoothly for head. Pull gather thread up tightly; then wrap thread around gathered fabric two or three times. Take a couple stitches in gathered area; then knot off thread.

6 Gather, stuff, and tie off small flesh-tone circle in the same way for the nose.

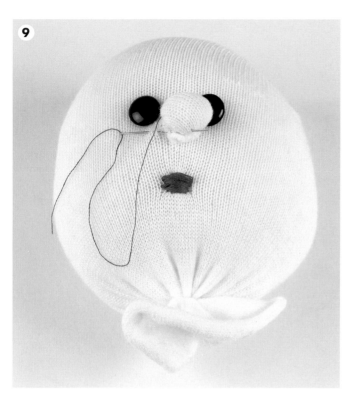

9 Slipstitch nose to face using matching thread. (Contrast thread was used here for clarity.)

10 Cut small slits ¼" (6 mm) in from both ends on one long side of the cardboard. This creates a loom to wrap yarn onto for the beard.

11 Place yarn end in the slit; then wrap around and around cardboard to next slit.

12 Using either the same yarn or matching thread, backstitch along top edge to secure the yarn.

13 Bend cardboard to remove the yarn beard. Pin the beard onto the head across face just below mouth. Slipstitch backstitched edge onto the face using matching thread.

(continued)

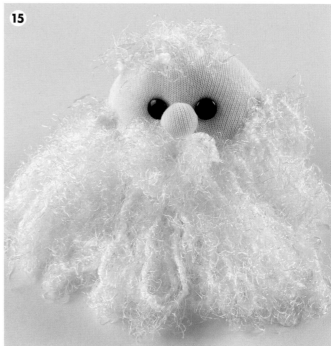

14 For mustache, wrap yarn around three fingers three times. Tie off in the center with another piece of yarn.

15 Slipstitch mustache to face right under the nose. Make another yarn bundle and slipstitch it to the face above the eyes for a bit of hair. Clip beard, mustache, and hair if desired or leave loopy.

16 Pull the toe section of the red sock over the head for a hat, allowing the bottom edge to curl up in a cuff. Slipstitch hat to the head.

17 Bend tip of hat down to one side. Sew bell to the hat tip.

18 Insert head into body and slipstitch to secure, allowing upper edge of body to curl, forming a collar.

19 Cut 1" x 14" (2.5 x 35.6 cm) strip of black felt for the belt. Cut two 2" x 4" (5.1 x 10.2 cm) rectangles for boots. Wrap belt around the doll from back around front. Sew ends together in back using matching thread or floss. Stitch the button to center front of the belt.

(continued)

20 Fold black felt rectangles in half, forming 2"
(5.1 cm) squares.

21 Use a running stitch to gather one end; knot but do not cut
off floss. Continue stitching up adjacent side, knot, and
cut off floss. Turn right side out.

22 Slide one boot onto a foot with seam to the back. Blanket
stitch (page 180) top edge to the doll leg. Repeat for
second boot.

23 Cut four green felt mittens using the pattern on page 183.
Blanket stitch around all outer edges; knot.

24 Slide mitten onto one doll hand. Continue blanket
stitch around base of mitten and doll arm. Repeat with
second mitten.

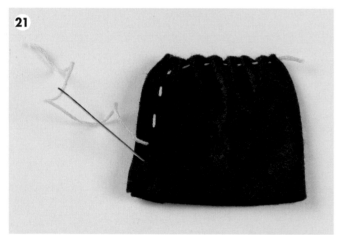

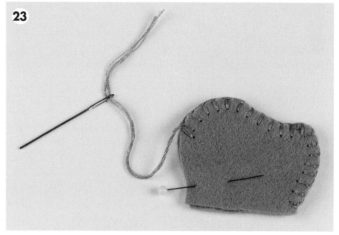

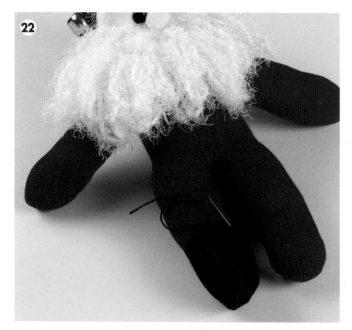

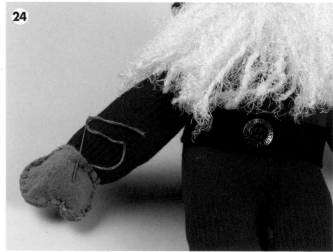

Monster Variation

You can make freeform sock dolls using mix and match socks, odd buttons, bits of felt, and trims for older children and even encourage children eight years old and up to make their own. A rainy afternoon is the ideal time to create snakes, monsters, or other simple freeform sock dolls.

The monster pictured here was made from a striped toe sock that was stuffed and stitched at the heel. The remaining length of the sock was stitched together to create a tail. Mismatched button eyes along with felt scraps create the face.

Pillow Doll

One of the simplest cloth dolls to make is a pillow doll. They're also incredibly versatile. Make one small enough to fit inside a pocket or large enough to be used as a bed pillow. The doll pictured is 6" x 8" (15.2 x 20.3 cm). Use fabric left over from decorating a child's room or clothing they have outgrown to make a very personalized pillow doll.

YOU WILL NEED

- ½ yd (0.46 m) fabric for body

- fabric for face and hands, 6" x 8" (15.2 x 20.3 cm)

- fabric for cheeks, 1½" x 3" (3.8 x 7.6 cm)

- fusible web, 1½" x 3" (3.8 x 7.6 cm)
(Note: Use lightweight fusible web if you will be machine stitching around cheeks and heavy weight if you choose not to sew cheeks on.)

- thin batting, 5" x 7" (12.7 x 17.8 cm)

- black thread

- pink or red thread for mouth and cheeks

- thread to match body and face fabrics

- stuffing

- disappearing marker

- basic sewing supplies

- iron

All seams are ⅜" (1 cm) unless otherwise stated.

1 Copy the basic pattern (pages 182-184). Cut one body back and front and four arm pieces from body fabric. Cut one face and four hands from face fabric.

2 Iron fusible web onto the wrong side of cheek fabric, following the manufacturer's instructions. Trace two cheeks onto the paper side of the fusible web. Cut out cheeks.

(continued)

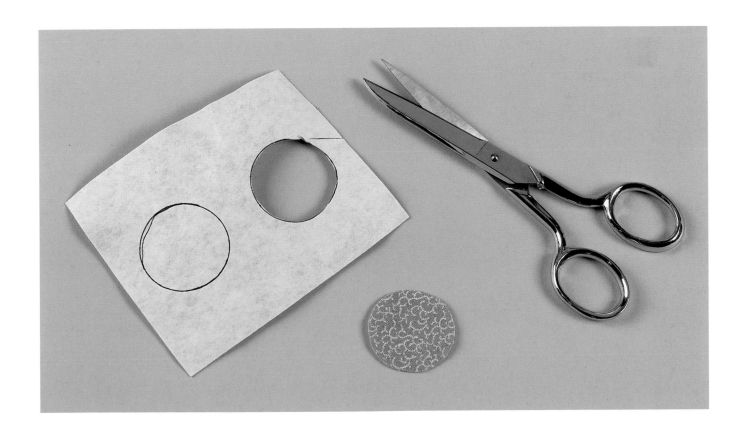

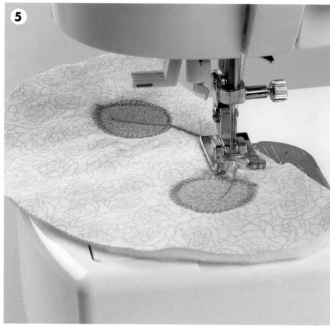

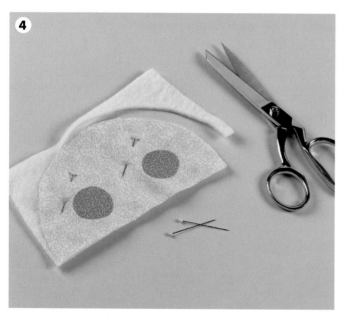

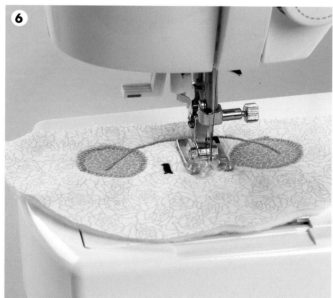

3 Peel off the paper backing on the cheeks and place onto face where indicated. Follow manufacturer's instructions on how to iron to attach.

4 Pin batting to wrong side of the face with attached cheeks. This will stabilize machine embroidery and keep face area smooth.

5 Zigzag stitch around cheeks using pink or red thread. If your machine has an appliqué or decorative stitch, you might want to try one of them. Using disappearing marker, draw on the smile line from the pattern. Use a narrow, tight zigzag (satin stitch) to stitch mouth.

6 Mark eyes using disappearing marker. Stitch eyes using a wide zigzag (satin) stitch and black thread.

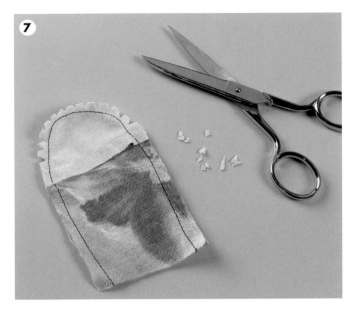

7 Sew a hand piece to the straight end of each arm. Pin arm-hand unit right sides together. Stitch down the side, around hand, and back up other side, leaving angled side open. Clip round ends, and turn right side out.

8 Pin open end of the arms to sides of the body front ½" (1.3 cm) down from top. Stitch ¼" (6 mm) in to secure arms to front.

9 Sew face to body front with arms. Pin right sides together; then stitch straight across.

10 Pin back to front, right sides together. Make sure arms are in toward the center of the body and will not be caught in the seam. Start stitching on straight bottom edge. Stitch around until 3" (7.6 cm) from beginning stitch; stop, back-stitch, and trim threads.

11 Trim curved edges as done with hands. Clip corners.

12 Turn right side out. Stuff loosely. Stitch opening closed.

Topsy Turvy Doll

Here is a unique doll with lots of play value. Flip the dress one way for a daytime, awake look, and then flip it the opposite way for a sleeping doll. Arms are inset into the body with heads on each end. Hair is done by creating a wig from felt and yarn.

YOU WILL NEED

- ⅓ yd (0.34 m) flesh-tone broadcloth

- ¼ yd (0.23 m) dress fabric

- ¼ yd (0.23 m) nightgown fabric

- 5" x 8" (12.7 x 20.3 cm) felt (same color as yarn hair)

- 10" x 3" (25.4 x 7.6 cm) fusible interfacing

- 52" (132.1 cm) 1½" to 2" (3.8 to 5.1 cm) wide pre-gathered trim

- 1 yd (0.91m) ¼" (6 mm) pre-gathered trim

- 1½ yd (1.37 m) ⅝" (1.6 cm) satin ribbon

- 1 oz. (28 g) sport weight yarn

- black, blue, pink, and white embroidery floss

- stuffing

- disappearing marker

- basic sewing supplies

(continued)

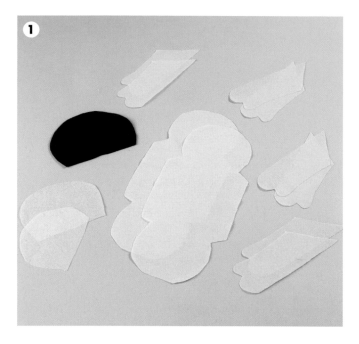

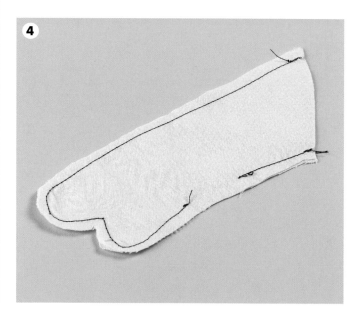

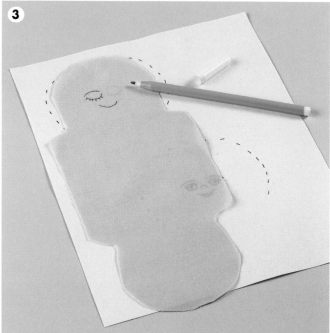

1 Trace the patterns on pages 185 to 187 and cut two head-bodies and eight arms from broadcloth. Cut two wig bases from felt.

2 Cut two pieces of fusible interfacing the same size as the head. Follow the manufacturer's instructions to fuse interfacing to wrong side of the heads. This is to stabilize fabric for embroidery.

3 Transfer faces to the heads. Place face patterns underneath one head/body piece, centering faces on the heads. Trace over outlines using a disappearing marker. If your broadcloth is thick, try taping pattern to a window with the fabric on top.

4 Sew all seams ⅜" (1 cm). Sew arms together leaving an opening on one side and at the top.

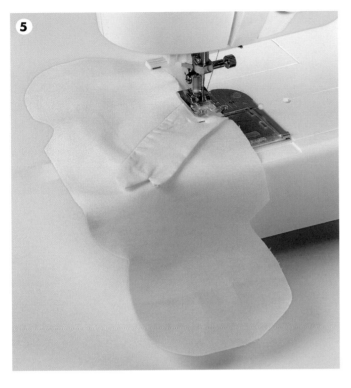

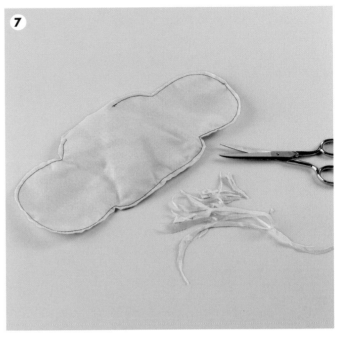

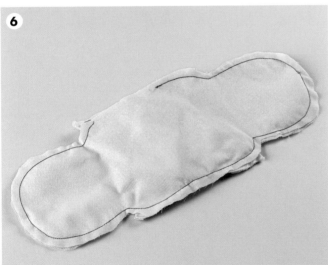

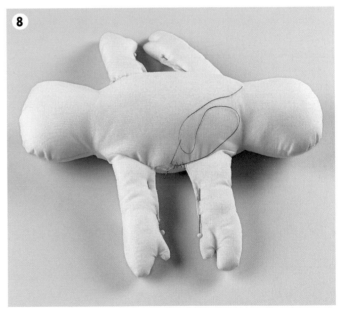

5 Sew arms to one body side along the top, diagonal edge.

6 Pin second body over the body with arms sewn on right sides together. Make sure arms are in toward center and sandwiched between sides of the body. Stitch around, leaving a 2" (5.1 cm) opening on one side.

7 Carefully clip and trim corners and curves.

8 Turn right side out and stuff. Ladder stitch openings in arms and body closed.

(continued)

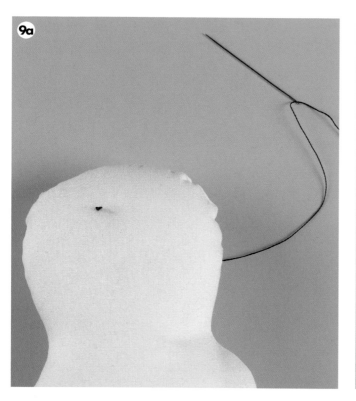

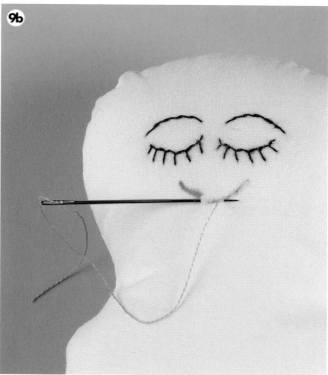

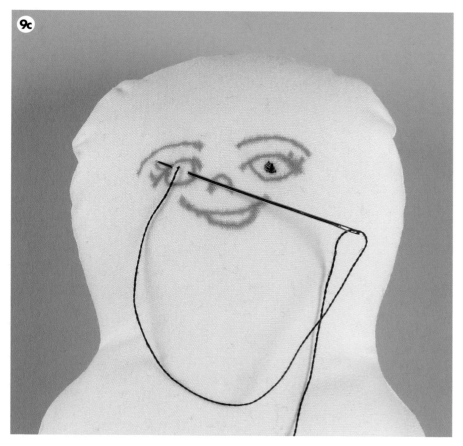

9 Embroider both faces, referring to pattern. Knot floss on backside of the head; then insert needle to front to start embroidery. Bring needle to back of head after finishing each area to prevent floss from shadowing through.

10 Create two wigs using felt base and yarn. (In sample, yarn was sewn to fabric so you can see it better.) Start sewing yarn loops to center of the felt. Wrap yarn around two fingers five or six times, slide off fingers onto felt, then stitch down centers. Repeat working around in a circle until felt is well covered.

11 Loops look more natural if they are slightly uneven.

12 Pin wigs to the doll heads. Slipstitch edge of wig to the front first, slightly gathering wig felt as you go. This will create added softness around the face.

13 Stitch all the way around the wig.

14 Trace the dress and nightgown pattern from page 188, and cut. Double-fold the fabric and place the pattern with center fold line on fabric fold. You will need a front and back of each fabric.

(continued)

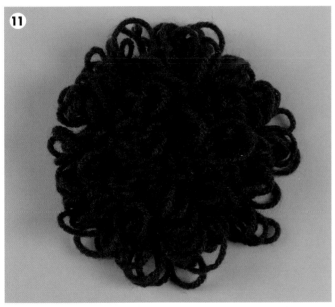

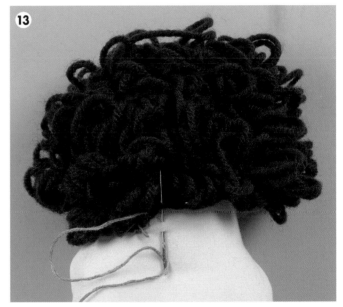

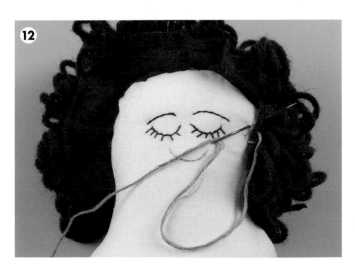

15 Cut a 3" (7.6 cm) slit from the neck down the center back of dress and nightgown.

16 Turn under raw edge on slit and stitch in place.

17 Sew trims to dress and nightgown hems and necks. Stitch 1½" to 2" (3.8 to 5.1 cm) trim to bottom of the dress and sleeves. Pin trims, right sides together, to sleeve and bottom hem edge with trim finished edge pointing in. Straight stitch along the trim edge. Pin trim to the wrong side of neckline fabric. Turn back trim cut edges next to back slit. Straight stitch into place. Flip trim over to right side, concealing raw edge. Repeat process on nightgown, using smaller trim at neck and sleeves only.

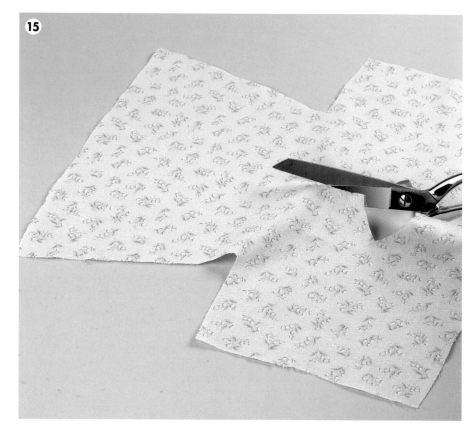

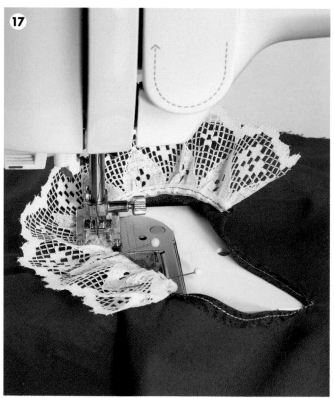

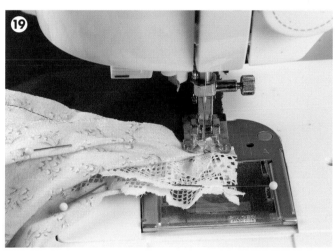

18 Pin, then stitch bottom hem of one dress side to one nightgown side, right sides together. Be sure the trim is sandwiched between the dress and the nightgown.

19 Pin sides and underarm seams right sides together on the dress. Along bottom hem, pin back nightgown edge. Stitch across sleeve trim to underarm/side seam corner; pivot. Stitch down the side and across trim sides. Clip diagonally into corner. Repeat for the other dress side and both sides of the nightgown. Turn right side out.

20 Slide dress onto the doll, putting nightgown on closed eye end. Use white floss to stitch top of back slits closed, forming a bow with floss if desired.

21 Either tie floss around ends of the sleeves or stitch and gather around the wrist areas. Tie ribbon around the dress waist in a bow. Add bows and additional trims as desired.

Ballerina Doll

Create this doll for the aspiring ballerina in your life. She is easily personalized with the child's hair and eye color. Button joints are suitable for children over three.

YOU WILL NEED

- ¼ yd (0.23 m) muslin or broadcloth in flesh tone
- ¼ yd (0.23 m) fusible interfacing (This is optional but will make your doll sturdier.)
- ⅓ yd (0.32 m) pink tulle
- 1½ yd (1.37 m) ⅛" (3 mm) pink satin ribbon
- premade pink ribbon rose
- four ⅜" (1 cm) four-hole white buttons
- black fabric marker
- red fabric marker
- blue (or other eye color) fabric marker
- pink colored pencil
- yellow (or other hair color) colored pencil
- stuffing
- pink embroidery floss
- strong thread such as carpet, or button
- sewing supplies to include pins, needles (one standard, one large eyed, and one longer with standard eye), sewing machine, scissors
- sturdy surface to tape pattern and fabric to or light box
- tape

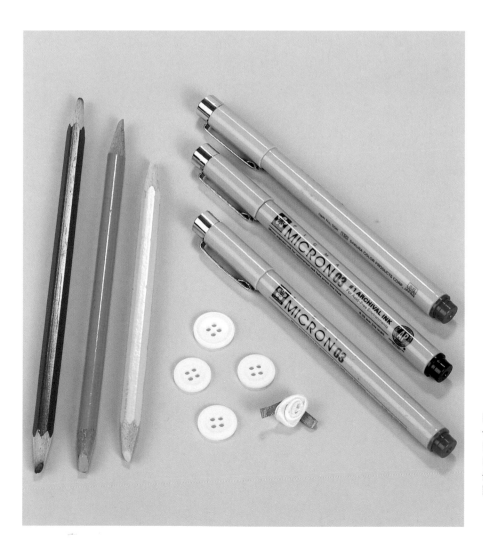

Permanent ink fabric markers with fine points are used for detail lines on the face and in the hair. Non-toxic colored pencils work fine for filling in color on the ballerina's leotard, cheeks, and hair.

(continued)

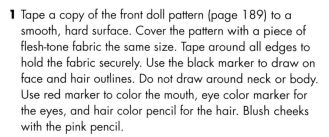

1 Tape a copy of the front doll pattern (page 189) to a smooth, hard surface. Cover the pattern with a piece of flesh-tone fabric the same size. Tape around all edges to hold the fabric securely. Use the black marker to draw on face and hair outlines. Do not draw around neck or body. Use red marker to color the mouth, eye color marker for the eyes, and hair color pencil for the hair. Blush cheeks with the pink pencil.

2 Draw around the body and just outside of the neck using pink pencil. Color in the body with pink pencil.

3 Draw and color the back of the doll using the pattern on page 190.

4 Draw on stitching lines with a disappearing marker.

5 Trace the arm and leg patterns (pages 189 and 190), and cut out four arms and four legs.

6 If desired, iron fusible interfacing to backs of all pieces, following manufacturer's instructions.

7 Hold body sections up to a light source (daylight window or light box) to align, and pin right sides together.

8 Sew around body, leaving a 1½" (3.8 cm) opening on one side. (Refer to pattern.) Pin the arms and legs right sides together. Stitch, leaving an opening to turn and stuff. Trim to within ¼" (6 mm) of the stitching line. Clip around curves and corners.

9 Stuff the body, arms, and legs. Ladder stitch all openings closed.

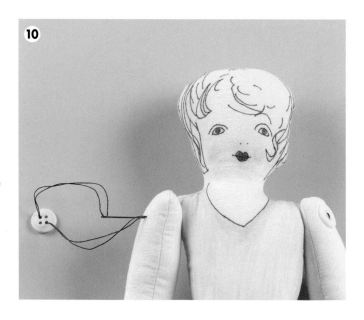

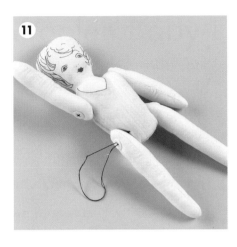

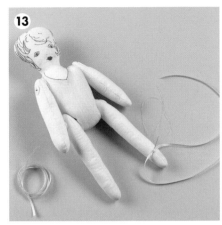

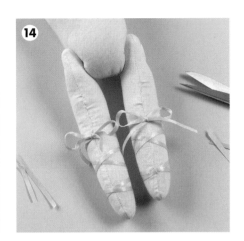

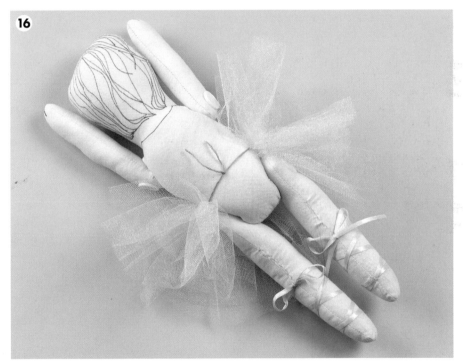

10 Attach the arms to the sides of the body using a long needle, double-strong thread, and two of the buttons. Make a knot about ¼" (6 mm) down from the top of the shoulder near the side seam. Push the needle through the body to the opposite side so the needle exits near the side seam and same distance down. Run the needle through the top of the arm and through a hole in a button. Bring the needle down through another hole in the button, back through the arm and body, then out the opposite side. Pull thread to snug the arm in toward the body. Run needle through remaining arm and button. Bring needle back down through button, arm, and body out to opposite arm. Go through arm again and out through an unused hole in button. Push needle back through another unused hole in button, through arm, body, and out of second arm and button. Use unused holes in second button, bringing needle out under arm near the original knot. Pull threads to adjust snugness of arms to body. Securely knot off thread.

11 Attach the legs in the same manner.

12 Color the bottom 1" (2.5 cm) of legs with the pink pencil to form shoes.

13 Cut 18" (45.7 cm) of pink ribbon. Pin center of the ribbon to the center front top edge of shoe. Stitch into place.

14 Wrap ribbon around to back of the leg; then stitch each side down to center back top of the shoe. Crisscross-wrap ribbon up leg; then tie a knot at the back of the leg. Trim excess ribbon.

15 Tie remaining ribbon around neck in a bow.

16 Cut tulle into two 6" (15.2 cm) strips. Use pink embroidery floss and a running stitch to gather tulle down the center of both strips. Stitch one strip; then add the next without knotting off. Gather the tulle up along the floss. Wrap around doll, adjust tulle, then pull floss ends together and knot.

17 Stitch ribbon rose to doll's head in the hair area.

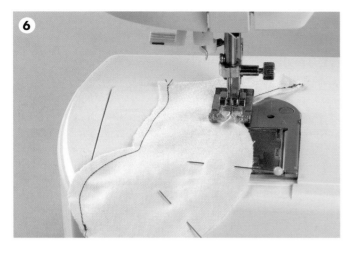

6 Stitch center back and center front of legs together. Stop stitching back seam at bottom of heel. Stitch front from top toe tip up to the opening for turning.

7 Pin, then stitch sole onto bottom of legs. Clip curves.

8 Turn legs right side out and stuff. Slipstitch opening at top of leg closed. Stitch large loops over end of feet to form toes.

9 Stitch darts in body front and back. Do not trim thread ends closely; allow a bit of excess at the beginning and end of darts, as darts may be stretched during stuffing; the extra thread can be pulled in if needed. Trim off the center of each dart after stitching.

10 Stitch the center front body together, ending at bottom point. Stitch the center back body together only to point just past third dart (refer to pattern).

11 Pin the body front to body back, matching up shoulders and bottom center points. Stitch, leaving neck open. Stitch down one side of neck, across shoulder, then down and around torso coming back up to second shoulder and side of neck.

12 Stuff body firmly, shaping tummy and seat area as you go.

13 Stitch belly button using double thread and a long needle, 3" (7.6 cm) or longer. Make a knot on the back at the top of the seat. Push the needle through the body to exit at the belly button. Take about ¼" (6 mm) stitch through front fabric; then reinsert needle to exit at knot on the back. Push the back and front toward each other with one hand while pulling on the thread. Stitch back and forth a few times. Stitch a knot on the back; then run the needle in through the body and out to hide thread end. Trim excess thread.

14 Transfer the face pattern (page 193) to center of front head using a dress maker's carbon or disappearing marker. Use a pin to poke small holes along facial feature outlines; then trace over with pen.

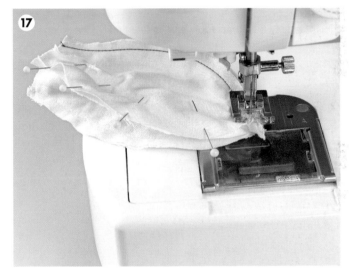

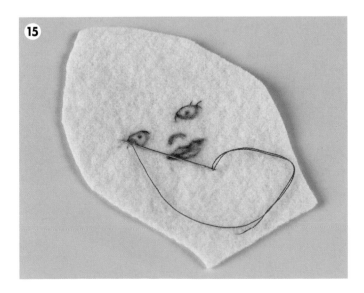

15 Embroider the face. Use a single strand of brown floss and a backstitch to create lash line and nose. Lashes are straight stitches of brown floss. Eyes are single-strand blue satin stitch with single-strand black satin stitch irises. A white French knot highlights the eyes. Lips are padded satin stitch. Stitch the top and bottom lip separately using a single strand of pink floss. Re-embroider lips using two strands of pink floss. Outline lips with backstitching. Rinse out marker or carbon.

16 Stitch darts in head front and back. Trim darts, as in step 9. Pin the head sides to front; stitch.

17 Pin the head back to head sides; stitch. Stuff head firmly and smoothly.

(continued)

Tara

Tara is a modern styled doll with jean Capri slacks, belted tunic top, sandals, and a painted face. Her construction is slightly different from previous cloth dolls with a shaped head attached onto a neck. If you would like, you can needle sculpt her face after painting, referring to pages 161-162.

YOU WILL NEED

- ⅓ yd (0.32 m) 36" (91.4 cm) wide wool felt
- 8" x 12" (20.3 x 30.5 cm) tunic fabric
- 11" x 7" (27.9 x 17.8 cm) Capri fabric
- 10" x 5" (25.4 x12.7 cm) brown felt for sandals
- 1 oz. (28 g) sport weight yarn for hair
- 14" (35.6 cm) of 1" (2.5 cm)-wide ribbon for belt
- small belt buckle
- string of beads or bracelet
- white gesso
- eye color paint in two shades
- mouth color paint in two shades
  (I used pure pigment colorants which make shading very easy.)
- detail paintbrush, small
- red fine-point permanent marker
- black fine-point permanent marker
- medium brown oil-based colored pencil
- cosmetic blush, optional
- disappearing fabric marker
- stuffing
- sewing thread to match skin tone, hair, and clothing
- sturdy thread such as carpet thread, Kevlar, or multiple strands of embroidery floss
- four flesh-tone buttons (two- or four-hole)
- one size 3/0 snap
- wire clothes hanger
- packing or masking tape
- basic sewing supplies

Wool felt is used to create this doll, making her sturdy yet shapeable. Wool felt is also easily dyed to create a variety of skin tones.

Variations on her clothing are easy. The tunic pattern can be lengthened to become a dress, shortened to become a blouse, or the sleeves lengthened to become a jacket. The Capri slacks can be lengthened to become slacks, cut as shorts, or widened to be pajama bottoms. Try using a bracelet as a necklace or tying on ribbon for a belt; the possibilities are endless.

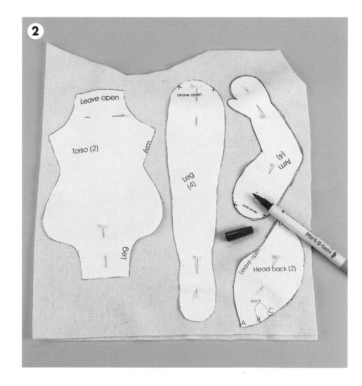

1 Copy all patterns (pages 195-197): torso, head back, face, arms, legs, tunic, pants, and sandals.

2 On felt that is folded in half, two layers, pin torso, back of head, arms, and legs, leaving ¼" (6 mm) in between pattern pieces. Trace around patterns with disappearing marker. Trace arms and legs twice.

(continued)

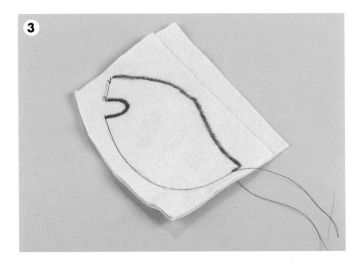

3 Sew around traced pattern lines, leaving openings as indicated on patterns. Cut out after stitching ⅛" (3 mm) past stitching line. Turn all pieces right side out.

4 Cut one face from the felt. Pin face pattern with eye, mouth, and brow holes cut out to face. Use disappearing marker to outline eyes, mouth, and brows. Remove pattern. Use marker to make two nostril dots ¼" (6 mm) apart and between ⅛" (3 mm) and ¼" (6 mm) above mouth.

5 Paint a layer of gesso on the mouth and eyes. Use the tip of a toothpick to smooth down fibers, particularly around the edges. Allow the gesso to dry.

6 Use black marker to draw irises on eyes, referring to face pattern below. Paint one side of the iris the lighter eye color and the other side darker. Make sure you paint both eyes the same so both eyes have light right or left sides. Draw a line across the mouth to indicate the top and bottom lips with red marker. Paint the top lip the darker mouth shade and bottom the lighter. Using the brown pencil, draw on brows with short strokes.

7 Outline the eyes and upper lid with black marker. Use a toothpick to add light and dark eye color lines to the irises. Dip end of the toothpick into paint; then stroke from the center outwards. Allow paint to dry.

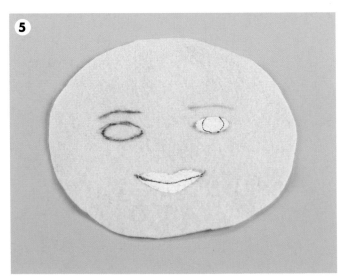

8 Outline the lips with red marker. Draw on sides of nose and U-shape, joining nostrils with brown pencil. Draw side of nose up toward the inner corners of eyes.

9 Using the brown pencil, shade around eyes, under mouth, and area just under nose center. Draw on lashes with black marker. (Refer to pattern.) Color in pupil with black marker.

10 Using a toothpick, highlight eyes with a dot of gesso on one side, same placement on both eyes. Mix two drops of gesso with a drop of water to thin. Brush a highlight across center of the bottom lip and a fainter, smaller one on the upper lip. Add another drop of water to gesso to thin more. Brush thinned gesso down center of nose, a small round on chin, and between brows and eyelid crease.

Allow gesso to dry.

11 Touch up any outlines or shading as needed. Brush cheeks with cosmetic blush, if desired.

Tip

Painting with gesso first provides a smoother foundation for the acrylic paint, and the features become more distinct. Detail lines can be drawn with permanent markers.

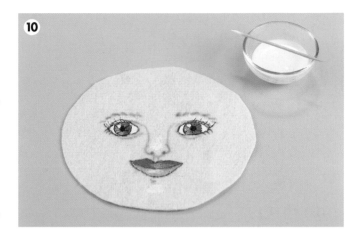

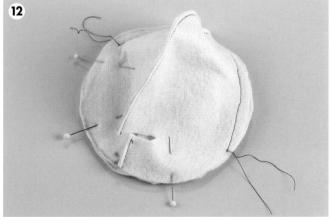

12 Pin face to back of the head, easing in fullness. Stitch around face. Turn head right side out.

13 Stuff all body parts. Ladder stitch tops of arms, legs, and neck closed.

(continued)

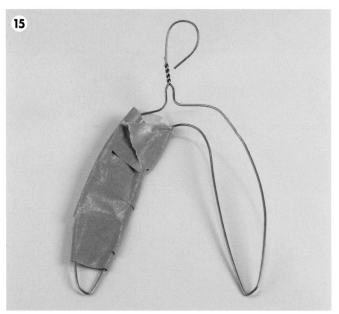

14 Place head on torso by inserting neck into neck opening in the head. Align face centered to shoulders; pin in place. Slipstitch head to neck, turning under the raw edge on the head neck opening as you go. (For extra security, stitch around twice.)

15 Create wig loom from a wire clothes hanger. Bend hanger as pictured; then wrap with packing or masking tape to help hold yarn in place.

16 Tie one end of yarn to side of wire loom. Wrap yarn in a figure eight around loom fingers until around 1" (2.5 cm) from the ends. Wrap yarn densely for best results. Tie off yarn.

17 Machine stitch down the center of the yarn wraps, backstitching at the beginning and the end. Clip knots; then slide off loom by slightly bending sides in toward the center. Repeat to make six lengths.

18 Stitch yarn lengths to the head for hair. Pin first section around the face, adjusting to create desired hairline. Slipstitch along machine-stitched line to attach. Pin, then stitch additional lengths to head, working around in a circle until a full head of hair is achieved.

19 Attach arms and legs as for the Ballerina Doll, step 10 (pages 36-37).

20 Soft-sculpt fingers and toes as for the Baby Doll, step 4 (page 41).

21 Fold foot at dash line on pattern. Stitch top of the foot to the leg to form a bend.

22 Cut two tunic and two facing pieces on the fold. Trim neckline on the front and front facing, as indicated on pattern. Slit the back and back facing 3" (7.6 cm) down the center. Sew tunic shoulder seams together. Sew facing shoulder seams together. Pin facing to tunic, aligning shoulder seams. Stitch facing to the tunic using 1/8" (3 mm) seam. Turn facing to the inside; press. Press 1/8" (3 mm) along bottom of the sleeves to inside; repeat to make a rolled hem. Topstitch hems in place. Sew underarm/side seams together. Press and stitch rolled hem along bottom. Hand-sew small snap to top of back opening.

23 Cut two pants on the fold. Sew center front and center back seams together. Press and hem bottom of each leg. Sew side seams together. Press, roll, and stitch top of pants at the waist.

24 Cut four sandal bases, two 1/2" x 3" (1.3 x 7.6 cm) heel strips, and two 1/4" x 9" (6 mm x 22.9 cm) straps. Fold the heel strip in place lengthwise, and pin to one end of one sandal base. Place the center of one strap in the center of the sandal base 1/2" (1.3 cm) from end opposite the heel strip.

25 Pin another sandal base on top, sandwiching in both heel strip end and center of the straps. Machine zigzag around outer edges of sandal base.

26 Cross straps at front; then bring ends through the heel strip in opposing directions. Straight stitch down center of the heel strip. Trim off excess strap. Repeat for second sandal.

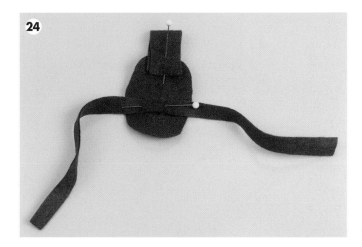

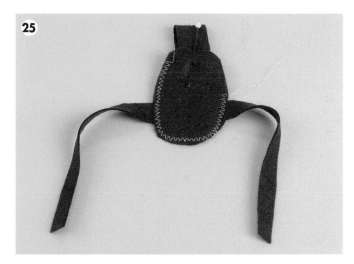

NATURE DOLLS

Probably the most primitive dolls were made of twigs and a scrap of fabric or whatever was around. The children who played with them loved them just as much as children today love their very fancy dolls with fashion clothes. Once you start making twig dolls, you will discover many items in your yard that will work with the design. It is interesting to see how a simple design idea can be tweaked to create some very special dolls. One special doll that you may have made as a child is the hollyhock doll. An open flower was used as the skirt and with a toothpick a bud was secured on top for the head. They would float in a bucket of water as though they were at a grand ball.

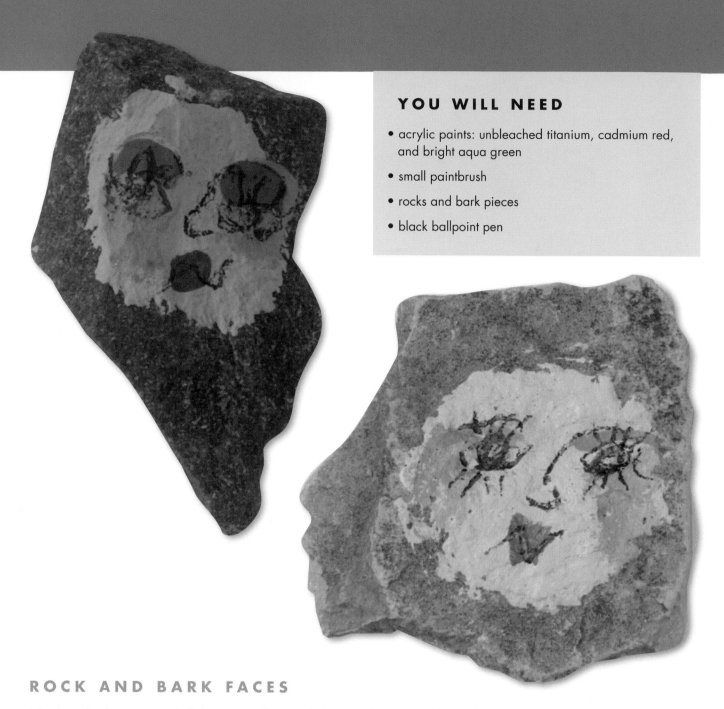

ROCK AND BARK FACES

Ideal rocks for nature doll faces are flat and thin. Collect suitable rocks along lakeshores, river beds, or other places and wash them in preparation for painting. One nice thing about dolls is that dimensions aren't very important, so a rock of almost any size will work. Use acrylic paint for the background colors and use a thin black pen to outline details.

Doll faces can also be made from tree bark. A piece of bark from a birch or apple tree will work just fine.

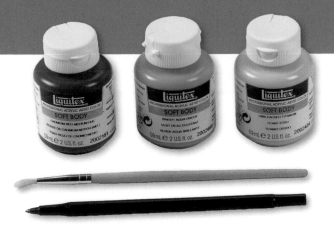

1 Paint a circle for the face using unbleached titanium.

2 Add some red to the unbleached titanium and paint the cheeks. Smear them a little so they blend in.

3 Add a bit more red and paint a dot for the mouth.

4 Add bright aqua green eye shadow.

5 With a black ballpoint pen, draw eyebrows, eyes, eyeballs, eyelashes, a nose, and a squiggle for the mouth on top of the red.

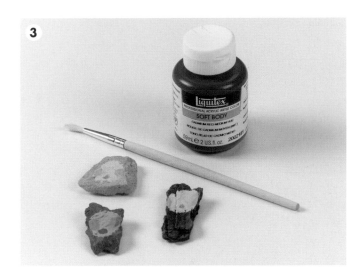

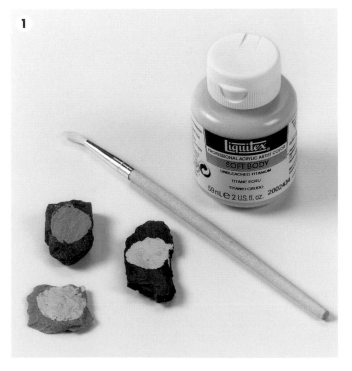

Sarah Jane Pin

Sarah Jane is a pin with a purpose. Because of her flat nature, she easily travels through the mail. She has gone from one person to another, and each person wore her to an event and then recorded it in a small journal that traveled with her.

1 Fold paper in fourths to make 2½" x 2¼" (6.4 x 5.7 cm) body. Glue bottom layers together and glue back down. Use clothespin to hold until dry.

2 Pull cotton ball apart and stuff it between layers of paper in the middle, and glue top layers to close. Use clothespin to hold in place.

3 String rabbit charm on a length of beading thread, loop, and tie off. The rabbit should hang into the center of the body. Glue thread in place where the head will go. Glue lower portion of the rock face and place over the rabbit thread so that half of the face is above the body.

4 Stitch on legs and arms with beading thread. Anchor thread at hip; string on five tube beads and one round bead. The round bead is the turn bead. Go back through the tube beads and anchor thread. Use the same method for the arms, anchoring at the shoulder and using three tube beads and a round bead for each arm.

5 Glue pin back to the back of the body near the top.

YOU WILL NEED

- a piece of flexible, organic looking paper 2½" x 9" (6.4 x 22.9 cm)
- one cotton ball
- one rock face
- four 4 mm off-white round beads
- sixteen 10 mm-long brown tube beads
- beige beading thread
- beading needle
- glue
- clip clothespins
- rabbit charm
- pin back

Twig Doll

With hair of roots and arms of twigs, this doll is simple enough for a child to make. Transforming such crude materials into a plaything or art object hints at the many other wonders nature provides. You'll never look at twigs the same way again.

YOU WILL NEED

- dried plant stalk with roots
- V-shaped twig for arms (try a small branch from an apple tree)
- strapping tape
- pruning shears
- 14" x 2" (35.6 x 5.1 cm) piece of fleece
- 1 yd x 1½" (0.91 m x 3.8 cm) brightly colored cotton fabric
- small black beads
- silver wish fob
- black beading thread and needle
- glue
- glue brush

1 The plant with roots, turned upside down, becomes the body and head of the doll.

2 Using the pruning shears, cut a V-shaped twig to form arms.

3 Position the V-shaped twig on the stalk and secure with strapping tape to form arms.

4 Wrap figure in fleece and glue the end flap.

5 Wrap figure with the cotton fabric and glue the end flap. Add a sash, 14" x 1½" (35.6 cm x 3.8 cm), and cut on the diagonal on the ends.

6 A necklace can be added using the black beading thread and needle. Stitch into the fabric at the back of the neck to secure. String enough black beads to reach the center of the doll, add silver fob, and the rest of the black beads. Secure thread at back.

Another Twig Doll

This doll was created with several twigs taped together to form body, arms, and legs. The body and arms can be wrapped first with knit fabric for sleeves. The lower body and legs are also wrapped in knit fabric. A belt was added with some beads and feathers. The head is half of a black walnut shell. Feathers and seashells complete the headdress, and a short necklace of beads is added at the neck.

Tip

Any sturdy root system will work. For a variation, try snap-dragon or pepper plant roots.

Corn Husk Doll

Corn husk dolls were loved by many country children. How ingenious their mothers were to make dolls with so few supplies. This folk art is still taught today.

YOU WILL NEED

- corn husks
- cotton balls
- thin twine or thread
- glue

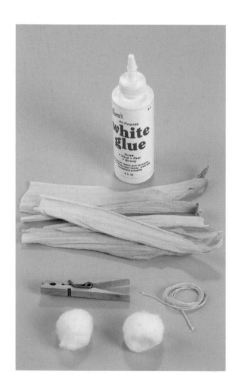

1 Cut husks from the cob and lay out to dry. When ready to use, soak in warm water until pliable, about one hour.

Husks must dry out first to prevent mildew.

2 Select six husks and tie then together, at the pointed end, 1" (2.5 cm) down from the point.

3 Turn the husks over the tied end, stuff with two cotton balls, and tie around to form the head and neck.

4 Find a husk about ¾" (1.9 cm) wide and wrap it over the top of the head to form a cap. Using the tails from the neck, tie the cap in place and trim. Add a ribbon-like piece around the neck.

5 Find three husks that are slender and about 9" (22.9 cm) long. Tie at one end, about ½" (1.3 cm) from the end, and braid to within ½" (1.3 cm) of the end. Tie. This braid is the arms.

6 Divide the doll's skirt in half from front to back and insert arms. When they are in place, wrap and tie a waist which will hold arms in place.

7 Find a husk that is about 1" (2.5 cm) wide and wrap it around the shoulders of the doll. Tie in place with the tails of the waist tie and trim.

8 Bring the hands together, glue, and clip with clothespin. This will make the arms curve and have a very natural look. Allow to dry a bit and remove clothespin.

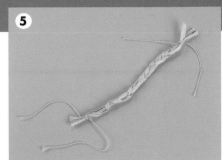

Tips

The corn silk can be dried and glued on the top of the head before the cap is put on. Other fibers could also be used for hair.

Alternatively, add a husk braid for hair.

If it is out of season for corn, try using tamale wrappers from the grocery store.

Simple clothes can also be added to the doll. Try an apron.

Make a male doll, forming legs by dividing the shirt in half and tying at the ankle.

Simple faces can be added with a marker, but make sure the husk is not damp or the marker may smear.

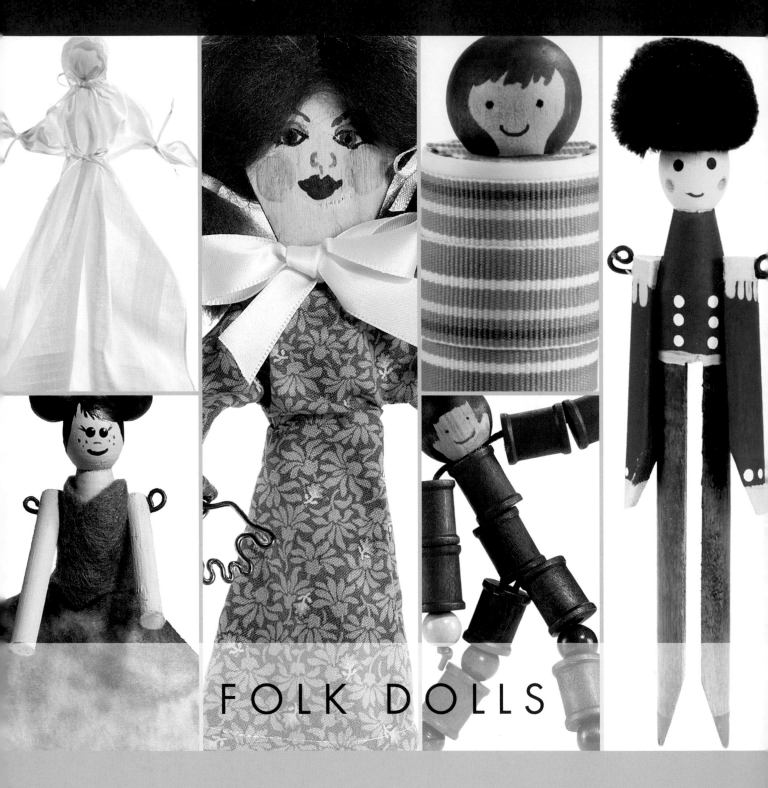

FOLK DOLLS

For centuries, parents have made dolls for their children, often out of handy materials they found in nature or cast-off materials left over from daily chores. Many of these dolls became traditions passed down through generations. These dolls are testament to the fact that, with just a simple human form, a child's curiosity and imagination can lead to hours of creative fun.

Spool Doll

Thrifty sewers have recycled their thread spools into dolls for many years. Spool dolls can be very simple, just a spool and a head, or more complex, stringing together spools and beads. Dress up spool dolls with bits of cloth, paint, dye, or markers. These dolls are simply charming.

Substitute any size spools, beads, or cording material. Check proportions on spools and beads by lining them up as you will be assembling later. Check to make sure cording material will pass through holes in both spools and beads.

1 Lightly pencil a simple face onto the ball knob. Make sure the flat side of ball knob is down.

2 Using permanent markers, color in hair and draw face details.

(continued)

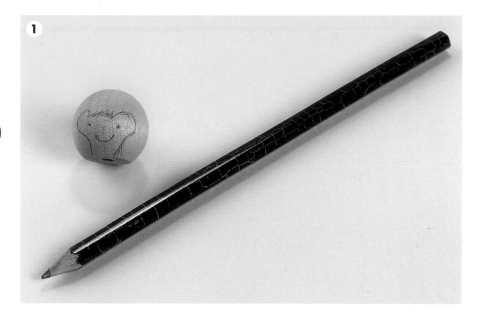

YOU WILL NEED

- ten ¾"x ⅝" (1.9 x 1.6 cm) wood spools

- one 1" (2.5cm) ball knob

- six 12 mm wood beads (four beads natural tone and two darker)

- 28" (71.1 cm) cording

- glue

- red, brown, and black permanent markers

- pencil

- painters' masking tape

3 Color spools using markers. Color five spools red. Color five spools and two natural-tone beads blue.

4 Refer to stringing diagram. Cut cording into 18" (45.7 cm) and 10" (25.4 cm) lengths. Fold 18" (45.7 cm) cording in half; then thread both ends through one red spool and one blue spool. Slide either 10" (25.4 cm) cording or pencil into loop at top of the red spool. Add one blue spool, one blue bead, one blue spool, and one dark bead to each end for legs. Tie loose knots on ends to temporarily secure. With 10" (25.4 cm) cording threaded under loop at top of the red spool, add spools and beads for arms. Thread two red spools and one natural-tone wood bead onto each arm. Tie loose knot on ends. Even up legs while pulling down so top loop is slightly inside center hole on the top spool. Knot end of leg cording tightly. Trim off excess cording. Adjust arms so they hang evenly at the sides. Knot arm cording ends tightly and trim off excess cording.

5 Glue ball knob head to top of the body. Use painter's tape to hold in place until glue has dried and set.

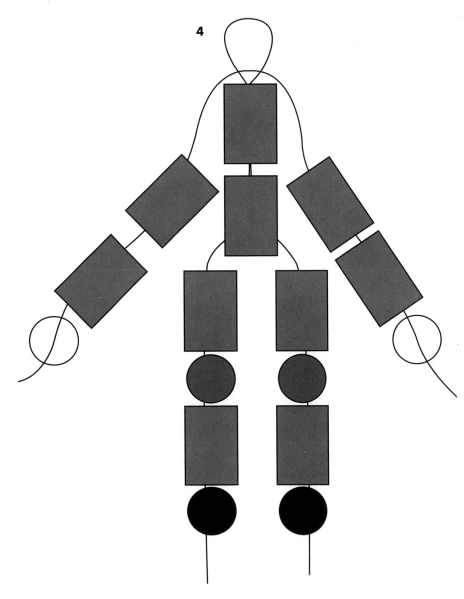

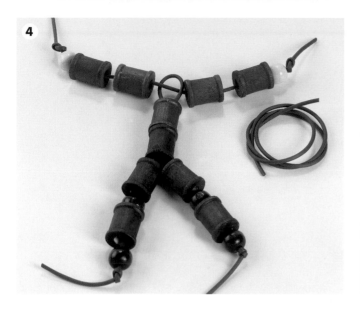

4

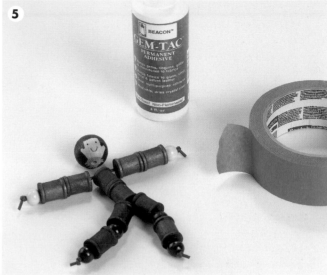

5

More Spool Dolls

Here is a simple variation. A ball knob head is glued to the top of the spool that has been wrapped with ribbon. Try making some of these using fabric scraps or leftover trims or yarns.

Spoon Doll

As with many folk dolls, spoon dolls were created out of materials on hand. Resourcefulness along with creativity resulted in a beloved toy for some lucky child. The originals did not have arms, only sleeves. Sometime later pipe cleaners were added for arms, but today we have plastic-coated wire to use to make sturdy arms.

1 Apply a coat of sealer to the back (domed side), of the spoon and allow to dry, according to manufacturer's instructions.

2 Copy the face pattern on page 198, or draw your own. Place transfer paper, carbon side down, onto back of the spoon. Align face pattern over transfer paper. Tape in place, if desired. Trace over pattern lines with a pencil. Remove pattern and transfer paper.

3 Using a very fine paintbrush, paint face. Paint nose, brows, and an arc around the top of the eyes brown. Paint the lips red and the center of the eyes blue or brown. Blush cheeks with thinned red paint dabbed on with a finger. Allow these paints to dry. Dot center of eye and paint on eyelashes with black paint.

(continued)

YOU WILL NEED

- wooden spoon
- 21" (53.3 cm) 18-gauge coated copper wire
- 14" x 8" (35.6 x 20.3 cm) fabric for dress
- 7" (17.8 cm) wool roving rope for hair
- 12" (30.5 cm) ⅛" (3 mm) satin ribbon for hair bows
- 12" (30.5 cm) ½" (1.3 cm) satin ribbon for neck bow
- acrylic sealer in matte
- small paintbrush
- acrylic paints in black, brown, red, and blue
- transfer paper
- very fine detail paintbrush
- pencil
- embroidery floss to coordinate with dress fabric
- basic sewing supplies
- wire cutters
- round-nose pliers
- glue

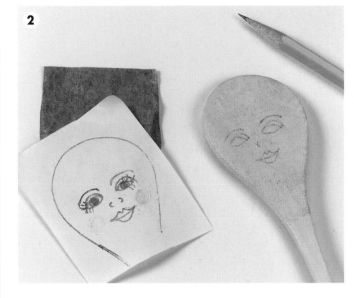

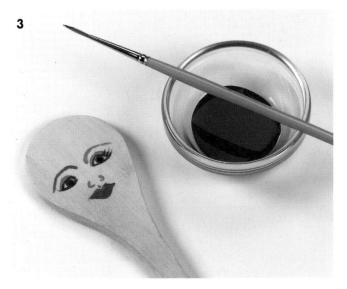

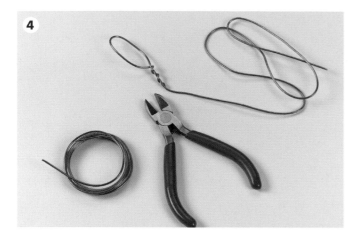

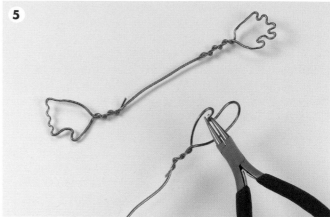

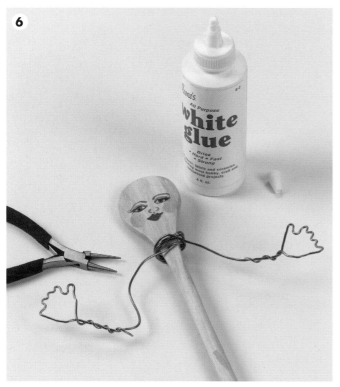

4 Cut 21" (53.3 cm) wire. Fold wire back on itself 3½" (8.9 cm). Using pliers, wrap the wire end around the wire base, forming a 1½" (3.8 cm) loop. Repeat on opposite end.

5 Bend a thumb shape using the round-nose pliers on one side of the loop. If desired, use round-nose pliers to create four more bends to represent ends of remaining fingers.

6 Wrap wire arms around the spoon three or four times. Place center of wire on the spoon; then wrap ends in opposite directions as tightly as possible. To tighten wire further, place tips of round-nose pliers over wire wraps on back, grip, and twist. Apply a dot of glue on wire wraps, if desired.

7 Stitch down center of wool roving.

8 Glue center of roving hair to back of the spoon with top portion rolling over top of the spoon. Allow glue to dry.

9 Cut two dresses using the pattern on page 198. Sew sleeve and side seams, right sides together.

10 Turn up and press small hems on sleeves and along bottom of dress. Sew bottom hem in place. Turn right side out.

11 Blanket stitch around sleeve hems using coordinating embroidery floss.

12 Slide dress onto doll; then blanket stitch around neck, pulling tightly as you stitch to gather fabric.

13 Tie 8" (20.3 cm) ribbons around sides of hair in bows. Trim hair ends, if needed. Tie ½" (1.3 cm) ribbon around neck in a bow.

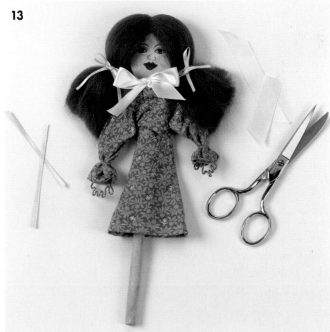

Clothespin Dolls

Clothespin dolls are one of our earliest and simplest dolls to make. Not only easy to create but easy on the budget, because they can generally be made with materials and scraps of fabric at hand.

Try all kinds of variations. Make ghost or witch dolls for Halloween, Mr. and Mrs. Santa Claus, brides and grooms . . . The possibilities are endless and a great project to involve the kids.

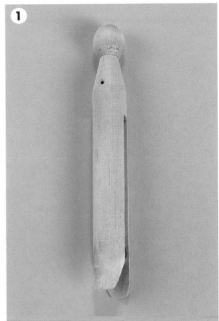

1 To make the basic body for a clothespin doll, start with round slotted clothespins purchased at the hardware store or your local craft store. Our clothespin is 4¾" (10.8 cm) long; this will be the head, neck, and legs of your doll. Start by measuring down from the top of the head (round part of the clothespin) approximately 1" (2.5 cm) and drill a hole through the clothespin using a 1/16" drill bit.

2 Cut the bottom (legs) of a clothespin off and use them as arms. These arms are more heavy and masculine, great for male figures. Cut them 2" (5.1 cm) long and drill a hole approximately an 1/8" (3 mm) down from the cut.

3 Use chopsticks to create a more slender female arm. Cut them 1¾" (4.5 cm) long and drill a hole approximately an 1/8" (3 mm) down from the cut.

(continued)

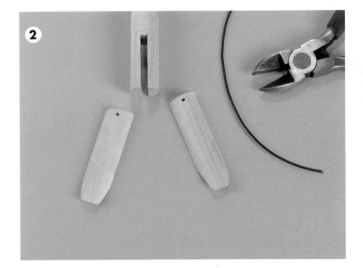

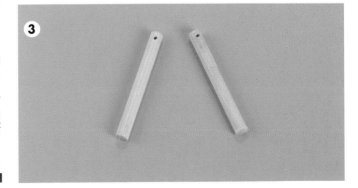

Tip

The dots for eyes can be made with the tip of a small craft paintbrush handle. Simply dip into paint and dot on the face. Using the handle tip of the brush will make the eyes the same size. If painting eyes are too scary for you, use gel pens.

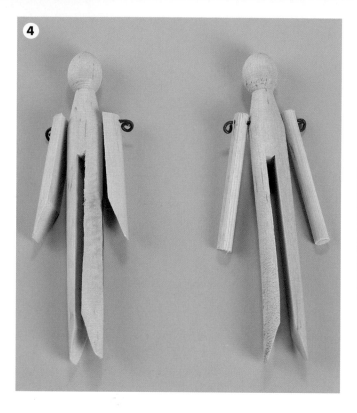

4

6

7

4 Using needle-nose pliers, curl one end of the 24-gauge wire. Then string the wire through an arm, then the clothespin and the second arm. Curl the wire to hold the arms in place. This is the basic Clothespin Doll body shown with both versions of arms.

5 Paint a circle on the front of the clothespin doll with flesh-colored craft paint. Allow to dry. Finish with eyes—simple dots are fine (see tip on page 75).

6 Make a mouth by painting a simple smile or two dots centered over one dot with a line through them. Use a red pencil to color the cheeks.

7 To make a traditional lady clothespin doll, start with the basic body, drill holes in clothespin and chopstick arms for wire. Glue wooden beads to the head for hair. Paint the face and hair. Paint on shoes. Cut a skirt from a 6" (15.2 cm) square of felt, using the pattern on page 199. Glue skirt on back of the clothespin with white glue. Cut a 1¾" x ½" (4.5 x 1.3 cm) band of felt for a shirt, and glue in place.

Tip

Embellish the skirt by cutting the edge with pinking shears. Add beads or small rickrack, if desired.

More Clothespin Dolls

To make a soldier clothespin doll—great as a Christmas ornament—start with the basic body and use clothespin arms. Paint the head with flesh-colored paint. For a jacket, paint the section below the head down to the split in clothespin red. Paint the legs blue, and paint the tips of the clothespin black for shoes. Paint a yellow band around the "waist" area for a belt. Paint flesh-colored hands, and red jacket sleeves. Top the sleeves with yellow epaulets. Paint the eyes, mouth, and cheeks in desired colors. Glue on a pompon for a hat. Attach arms when dry.

For a fairy clothespin doll, start with basic body and chopstick arms. Paint the head with flesh-colored paint. For clothing, use small paper flowers from your craft store as a dress, smaller flower petals for hair, and leaves as wings. Paint the face and end of the chopsticks (arms) with flesh-colored paint. Top off with an acorn cap.

Yarn Doll

These quick and easy dolls are ideal for using up bits of leftover yarns and can easily be adapted in a smaller size for ornaments. Mix and match colors, change length of hair, and even glue on a face if desired.

YOU WILL NEED

- 2 oz. (57 g) main yarn color
- ¼ oz. (7 g) yarn for hair
- 12" x 8½" (30.5 x 21.6 cm) sturdy cardboard
- fabric glue

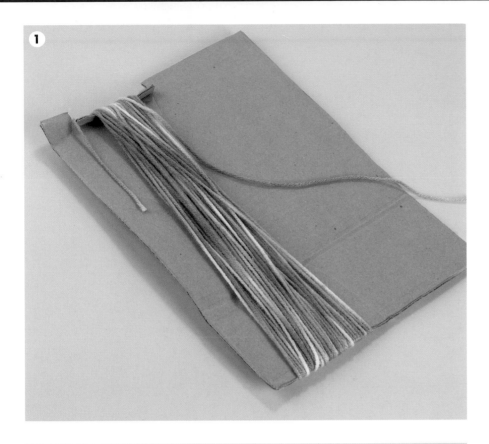

1 Cut a small slit on one end of the short side of cardboard. Insert end of main yarn into this slit to temporarily hold it. Wrap yarn around the long side of the cardboard fifty times.

2 Tie a length of yarn around yarn wraps with a secure knot. Slide yarn off cardboard by slightly bending cardboard.

(continued)

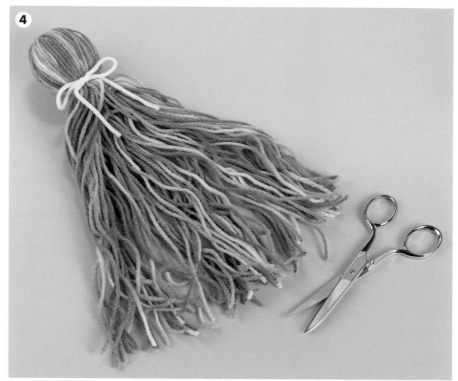

3 Wrap main color yarn into a 1½" (3.8 cm) ball to help form the head.

4 Cut bottom loops on yarn bundle created in steps 1 and 2. Open up yarn wraps; then slide yarn ball in center next to where large bundle is tied off. Smooth yarn over ball; then tie off underneath with a length of yarn.

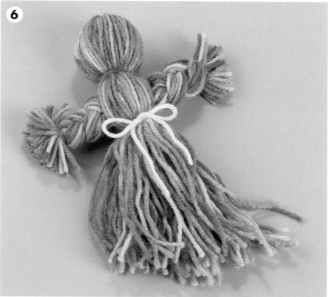

5 Wrap main yarn around cardboard thirty times along same length as in step 1. Use a length of yarn to tie off one end of yarn bundle. Cut loops on the opposite end. Do a simple over-under braid down length of yarn bundle. Tie off end of braid with a length of yarn. Trim ends evenly.

6 Open up yarn bundle with head; slide arms in next to head. Center arms to head. Tie a length of yarn around body directly underneath arms.

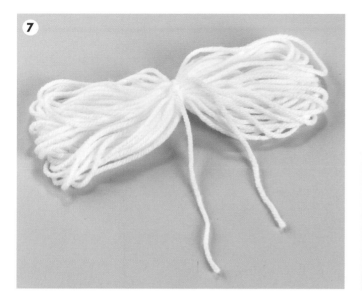

7 Wrap hair color yarn around shorter width of cardboard thirty times. Remove yarn from cardboard keeping bundle together. Using a matching length of yarn, tie around center of bundle.

8 Cut loops open and spread out hair.

9 Glue center of hair bundle to top of head using fabric glue.

Hankie Dolls

Hankie dolls were also called church dolls or pew dolls because they were first made for children to play with during church services. The idea was that if the doll was dropped, it wouldn't make noise.

The dolls have been made in various ways and we will show you two different ways. Similar dolls were made from lacy women's hankies and given to a newborn baby girl with the intention that she would later carry it as her bridal hankie.

(continued)

YOU WILL NEED

- Styrofoam ball 1¼" (3.2 cm) diameter

- one hankie 15½" (39.4 cm) square

- ⅛" (3 mm) wide pink satin ribbon

- 6" x 1" (15.2 x 2.5 cm) gathered eyelet

- glue

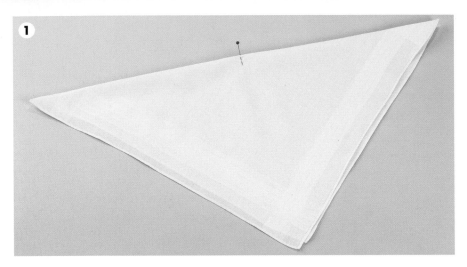

Version 1

1 Fold hankie diagonally in half and find the center of the folded side.

2 Place the ball in the center and wrap the sewing thread tightly around several times to form a neck. Tie a knot and trim ends.

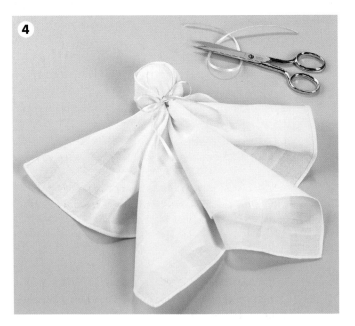

3 Pull up a small fold from the back and wrap it around the top of the ball to form a cap. Wrap sewing thread around neck to hold in place.

4 Wrap ribbon around the neck and tie into a bow.

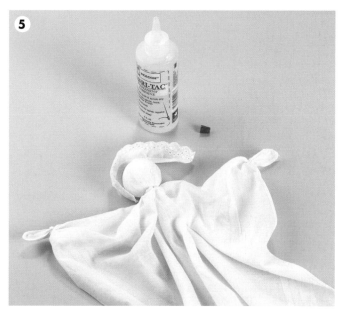

Version 2

1 Lay out hankie and find the center of one side.

2 Put the ball in the center of hankie edge and roll it down until the hankie covers the ball and edge can be caught in the tie.

3 Wrap the sewing thread around the ball to form a neck. Tie thread and trim ends.

4 Pull out the corners of the hankie that are along this same edge and wrap sewing thread around each to form wrists. The hand part will be about 2" (5.1 cm) long.

5 Put eyelet around head to see where the cap will go, and then glue the eyelet in place.

6 Tie pink ribbons around the neck, wrists, and very loosely around the middle to create a waist.

Garden Glove Doll

Cotton garden gloves come in a wide variety of colors and prints, so you have lots of choices when you select gloves to transform into dolls.

YOU WILL NEED

- one garden glove
- patterned cotton fabric 16" x 4½" (40.6 x 11.4 cm)
- solid fabric 16" x 2" (40.6 x 5.1 cm) or gathered eyelet trim 16" x 1½" (40.6 x 3.8 cm)
- 1 yd. (0.91 m) two-ply variegated fingering yarn in hair colors
- red perle cotton or craft thread
- large tapestry needle
- two 4 mm round black beads
- beading needle
- black and white thread
- fiberfill
- glue
- hemostat or other stuffing tool

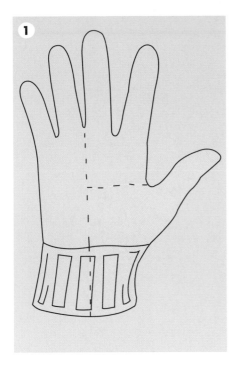

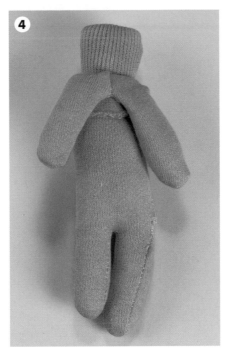

1 Cut one glove following the diagram. The little finger and the ring finger with cuff become the legs, body, and head of the doll. The index finger and middle finger become the arms; the thumb with cuff is discarded.

2 Turn the legs, body, and head section inside out and sew a very narrow seam along the cut edge. Turn right side out and stuff.

3 Fold the top of the cuff inside, leaving 2" (5.1 cm) for head and face. Slipstitch the top closed.

4 Stuff the arms and fold over the cut edge. Hand-sew the arm piece at the back of the neck. The arms will pull forward when put into the arm holes of the dress.

5 Embroider a mouth with red yarn. Take one long stitch and then a very small stitch in the center of the long stitch to hold it down; pull to form a smile. Add black beads for eyes.

6 To make the dress, press under ½" (1.3 cm) hems on the long edges. Lap one folded edge over the raw edge of the trim and stitch. The trim will look like an underskirt.

7 With right sides together, stitch a ⅜" (1 cm) back seam. Cut a 1" (2.5 cm) slit in both sides, ½" (1.3 cm) down from the top for the arm holes.

8 Run a basting stitch around the top, ⅜" (1 cm) down from the top. Gather the dress to fit the neck of the doll. Slip over the doll's head with arms in the holes and fasten the dress to the doll with the thread used to gather. Hide stitches in the gathers.

9 Thread yarn onto the tapestry needle and make large, unruly French knots (page 181) all over the top of the head. Glue a fabric bow to the back of her head.

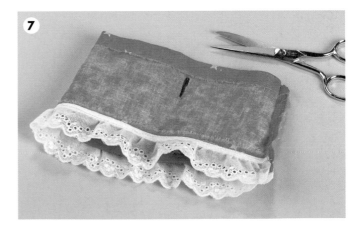

PAPER DOLLS

Throw out your old notions about paper dolls. Some paper dolls are made for display and can be used in scrap books or just to dress up your space. Others are definitely meant to be played with. They can have jointed, moveable arms and legs, or they can hold hands in a long garland. You have lots of options for paper doll faces: hand-drawn features, photocopies, or faces cut from magazines. You can also get creative with their hair. Paper choices are endless, and painting your own paper for your dolls makes them very personal.

PAPER FACES

There are quite a few ways to make paper faces for your dolls. Remember that a face does not have to be realistically proportioned with artistically rendered features. Some of the most interesting results can be achieved when you allow yourself to be creative and spontaneous.

Blind Portrait

This is a liberating, creative exercise that allows you to escape the confines of the expected and move beyond judgment. Judgment stifles creative energy; allowing yourself to create without judgment is a gift to you and allows latent talents to emerge. Please do share this technique with others; it is fun and delightful to do with a group. You and they will be amazed at what is created. There is a charming honesty to these portraits. You will find that they often reflect your mood and contain the essence of someone's personality.

You will need a stack of paper; inexpensive copy paper is fine, a pen, pencil or marker that will draw smoothly. The first few times you go through this exercise it is helpful to have another person guide you, after that it is easy to do on your own.

1 Place your paper on a flat surface. Put your pencil to the paper, close your eyes and begin. Do not open your eyes or lift your pencil from the paper until you have finished.

2 Starting at the right outside point of the eye, draw the bottom of the eye and then the top. Continue around to draw the eyebrow and then a nose.

3 When you think you are about even with the right eye draw the left eye starting at the inside corner and then around. Continue and draw the left eyebrow and around the left side of the face. Draw the mouth in the middle of the chin and continue on to where you think the right ear would be.

4 From here draw the hair around the top and part way down the left side of the face.

5 When the drawing is complete, open your eyes and fill in the face with the colored pencils.

2

3

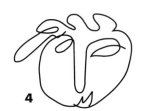
4

Ancestors and Family Photos

Use your computer's photo editing program to adjust sizes before printing, or use a photocopier to shrink or enlarge already printed photos. Mount the photos on stiff paper. Color black-and-white photos with colored pencils, if desired.

Embossed Toilet Tissue

1 Select a rubber stamp face with well-defined features. Use three or four pieces of inexpensive toilet paper. Place the layers of paper over the stamp. Wet and tap down with your fingers to remove any air that is trapped. Then using a cotton swab, press down around the features. Let dry on the stamp.

2 Remove the toilet tissue when dry, and trim. Apply color to this imprint using chalk and a dry eye shadow applicator or cotton swab. Colored pencils can be used to add details.

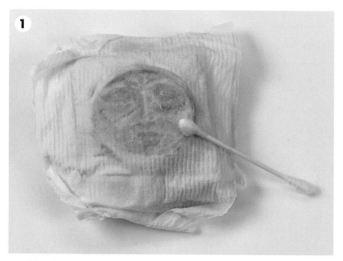

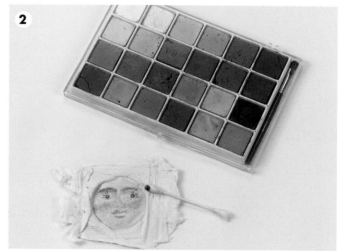

Rubber Stamp

Using a rubber stamp is probably the fastest and easiest way to create a face. Stamp on white paper using a brown or black ink pad. Let dry. Color with colored pencils.

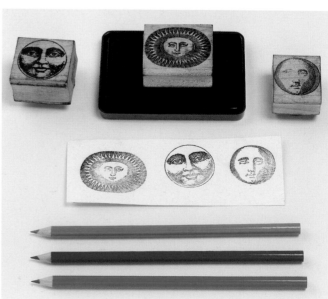

Creative Paperclay and Push Mold

There are many different push molds available. Follow the directions on the Paperclay package and the push mold to create doll faces. Let dry. Using acrylic paint, color the faces with unbleached titanium, cadmium red, and bright aqua green. Use a black ballpoint pen for details.

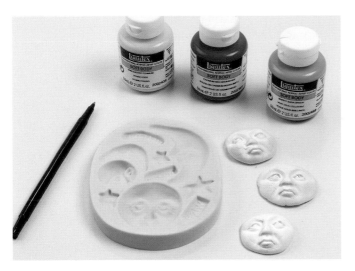

Hair Techniques for Paper Dolls

Yarns of all kinds work well for doll hair. Loosely twisted, thick-and-thin yarn (right) might look like colorful dreadlocks. Eyelash yarn (below, left) can mimic wild, unruly tangles. Raffia, used in the creative headdress style (below, right), can be braided, spiked, knotted, or coiled. Also try curling ribbon or curly paper shreds intended for gift bags. Colored paper run through a paper shredder will give you interesting strands and paper bits, too.

PAINTING PAPER

There are many art papers available for making paper dolls, but also consider painting plain paper or cardstock. These methods can give your paper dolls unique looks.

Encaustic

Encaustic is done using color crayons and cardstock. The work is done on a hot plate (the kind you use for a buffet to keep dishes warm).

1 Place the paper on the hot plate and spread pieces of crayon on top. Large pieces take longer to melt but when they have, you can make them run in the direction that you want. Small shavings are also very effective. Try some of each on your first piece. This is a perfect way to use up old broken crayons.

2 When the piece is the way you want it, remove from hot plate and let dry. Caution: The edges and center of the hot plate will be very hot.

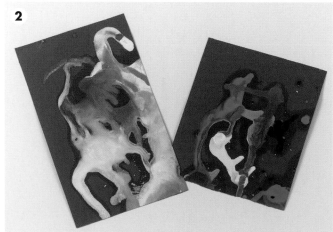

Wax Paper

1 Cut a piece of wax paper twice the length of the desired finished print. On one half of the wax paper, dribble paint colors.

2 Fold the other half of waxed paper over the painted side and move the paint around with your hands to create wonderful mixtures of color.

3 Open the waxed paper and place the paper to be printed on top of the paint and press down.

4 Remove the print. Create a second print from the other side of the waxed paper. Set aside to dry.

Tip

Don't throw out the waxed paper—it is a beautiful mix of colors with the light coming through. You will find another use for it.

Clear Fingernail Polish

The clear fingernail polish print is one of my favorites.

1 In a shallow pan with a lip, lay a piece of dark cardstock and cover with water. Drop several drops of clear fingernail polish on top of the water. It will look like an oil spill.

2 Using both hands, carefully remove the paper from the water, lifting the paper straight up. Do not allow the water to run off the paper, as the "oil spill" will disappear. Place on a flat surface to dry.

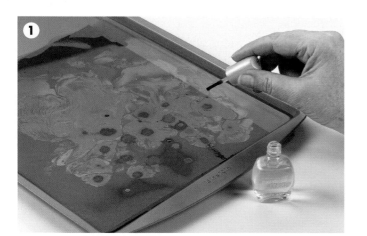

Plastic Wrap

Wrinkled plastic wrap makes wonderful designs on paper.

1 Wet watercolor paper with a spray bottle or under the tap and place on your work surface covered with paper.

2 Use fluid acrylics or watered down regular acrylics. Add paint.

3 After the surface is covered with the paint and very wet, cover with wrinkled plastic wrap and press down. Allow to dry before removing plastic wrap.

Tip

Try the same technique with bubble wrap.

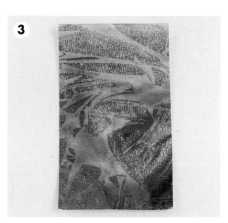

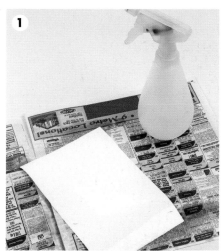

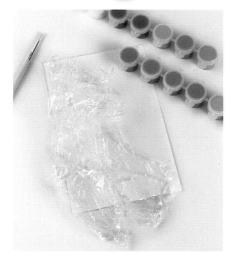

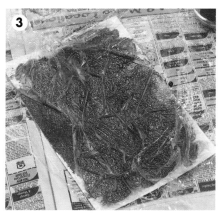

Little Dolls That Move

Paper dolls are pretty simplistic, but you can have a lot more fun with them if they can move. These dolls are made from painted paper. Arms and legs are attached with tiny brads so you can pose the dolls in lots of positions. For even more options, create your own patterns and give your paper dolls more joints: knees, elbows, feet, hands, and neck.

YOU WILL NEED

- small piece of painted paper
- brads
- face rubber stamps
- stamp pad
- white paper
- colored pencils
- white glue
- awl

Brads are very easy to use. They come in many sizes and colors and are reasonably priced. A small hole is made in the paper at the joint location with an awl or tiny-hole paper punch. The brad is pushed into the hole and then opened in the back. Brads can also be used at knee and elbow joints to give more movement, especially for a larger paper doll. Eyelets, buttons, or a piece of yarn can also be used to connect joints and allow movement.

1 Trace the pattern pieces (page 199) on the back of the painted paper. Reverse one leg and one arm in order to have a right and left arm and leg. Cut out.

2 Make small holes in the shoulders, top of arms, hip, and top of leg with the awl. Attach the arms and legs with brads pushed through the holes.

3 Stamp a face on the white paper and color with the colored pencils. Cut out the face and glue it to the head.

Tip

Embellish by adding threads to one hand. Thread some glitzy thread on a needle and poke through the doll's hand. Tie a knot to hold.

Paper and Stick Doll

This doll could be used as a decoration on a gift package. Her face is a blind portrait (page 90). If you make some extra faces ahead of time, you could choose one that suits the occasion or the recipient of the gift.

YOU WILL NEED

- 8½" x 5½" (21.6 x 14 cm) textured paper
- 4½" x 1½" (11.4 x 3.8 cm) decorative paper
- two 12" (30.5 cm) twigs
- blind portrait face
- assorted 14" (35.6 cm) pieces of yarn
- three small buttons
- bone folder
- white craft glue
- glue brush
- pruning shears

1 Fold textured paper in thirds. Run a bead of glue down the inside folds and place twigs in the folds.

2 Add more glue around the twigs and fold paper over the twigs, lapping in the back. Glue back pieces together.

3 Add decorative paper panel in the center front.

4 Glue on blind portrait face and buttons.

5 Tie yarns around one arm.

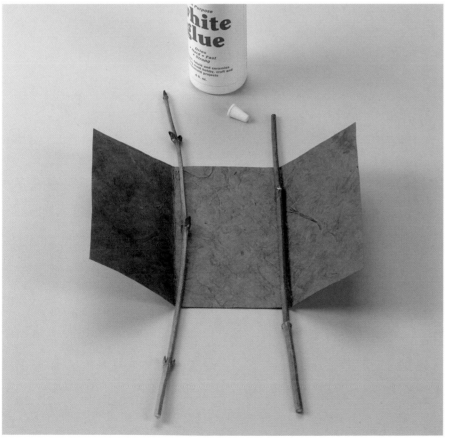

Tip

Cut straight, sturdy twigs with the pruning shears and remove leaves. Cut several in the winter when there are no leaves and you can see the branch better.

Tall Paper Doll

This paper doll is fun to make in multiples of different heights to display together on a shelf. Using gem tone papers and different face stamps, you can create the three wise men for a holiday decoration. As a vacation memento, her open coat might reveal ticket stubs, stamps, coins, small maps, or other flat memorabilia.

Tip

A bone folder is a wonderful tool for making crisp folds. Simply slide the flat side of the round end along the fold. The edge of the bone folder is good for scoring a line before you fold.

YOU WILL NEED

- 12" x 10½" (30.5 x 26.9 cm) rectangle white posterboard
- 2" x 2" (5.1 x 5.1 cm) square white posterboard
- assorted papers in the same color family
- 1¾" (4.5 cm) embossed face
- colored pencils
- hand-shape paper punch
- eyelash yarn
- variegated silk ribbon, ½" (1.3 cm) wide
- bone folder
- white glue
- glue brush
- ruler
- charm

1 Fold the large piece of posterboard into three sections so the middle is 5" (12.7 cm) wide, left side is 3" (7.6 cm) wide, and right side is 2¼" (5.7 cm) wide. Crease the folds well with the bone folder.

2 Measure 4" (10.2 cm) down on each front section at the center edge. Fold on a line from that point to the top of the side fold to form the lapels.

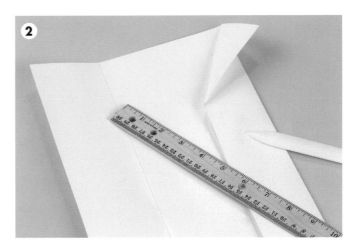

3 Cover all surfaces of the posterboard with the assorted papers, using the glue brush to smooth out glue. Fold down the lapels.

4 Wad up the eyelash yarn and glue it in the center of the middle section.

5 Glue the embossed face to the middle of the yarn. Allow to dry.

6 Cover the small posterboard square with paper for the arm. Make one hand punched from a scrap of sturdy paper and color it to match the face. Glue near edge of the arm and glue the arm at the front opening.

7 Glue ribbon along the center edges and the end of the arm.

8 To make a ribbon tassel, cut four 5" (10.2 cm) pieces of ribbon. Fold three pieces in half and tie together at the middle with the fourth piece. Glue the tassel at the neck of the front piece.

9 String a charm on a ribbon or piece of yarn, and tie around the arm.

Punch, Judy, and Lulu Puppets

These little dancing puppets make use of recycled materials. Empty toilet tissue rolls decorated with paper become their bodies. Creative Paperclay is used to make their faces (page 93.) Movement is controlled by sticks inserted into the backs of the dolls. You can have hours of fun making up little skits with your paper puppet dolls.

1 Cut two paper rolls: Judy 3½" (8.9 cm) and Lulu 2" (5.1 cm). The roll for Punch is not cut.

2 Using glue and glue brush, attach patterned paper to each paper roll.

3 Put one staple in the top of each roll to close.

4 Make a hole in the center back of each puppet to accommodate the chopstick.

5 Using the awl, make holes in each puppet at the shoulders and bottom front.

6 For arms and legs, glue three layers of card stock together. When dry, cut arms and legs in desired sizes for each puppet.

7 Using the awl, make a hole in the top of each arm and leg.

8 Open jump rings with pliers, and attach the arms and legs to each puppet. Close jump rings.

9 Paint Paperclay faces and glue one to the center of each puppet.

10 Glue pieces of yarn on the puppet heads for hair.

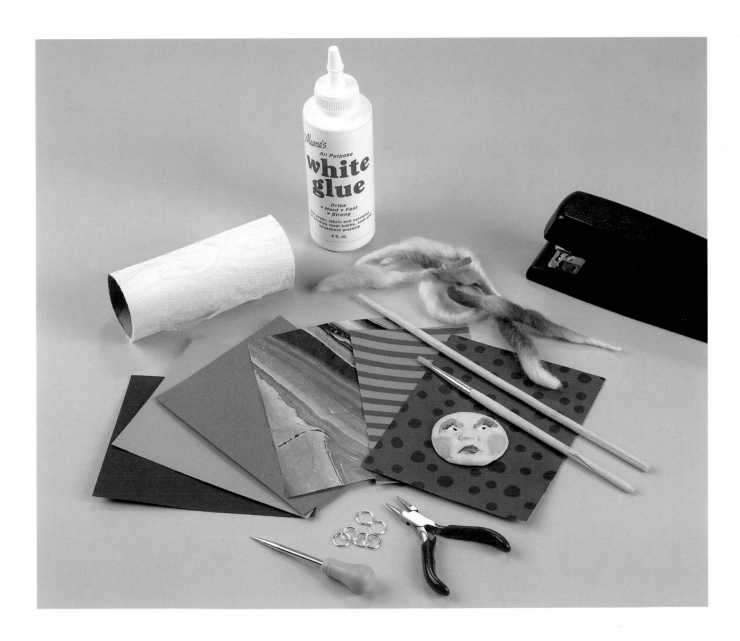

Paper Doll Chain

Everyone probably has folded and cut paper doll chains sometime in their childhood. They were so much fun to cut out of special paper. There are many specialty shops that carry beautiful papers, and that's where the paper for these dolls came from. Faces of family members give this project a personal twist.

YOU WILL NEED

- one piece of specialty paper cut to 11" x 6" (27.9 x 15.2 cm)
- paper lace motifs
- small buttons
- four faces
- bone folder
- glue
- glue brush

Tips

The chain can stand on its own, be tucked into a mirror frame, or be used as a decoration on a Mother's Day gift. You could also make a chain with faces on the back and wrap it around a clear vase.

1 Fold paper in fourths using the bone folder to make sharp creases.

2 Trace the pattern (page 200) on the wrong side of the paper.

3 Cut out pattern, being careful not to cut connections on the folds.

4 Cut small lace motifs for the dolls that will have girl faces. Glue lace to girl dolls.

5 Cut out faces and glue to the dolls.

6 Glue small buttons to the front center of the boy dolls.

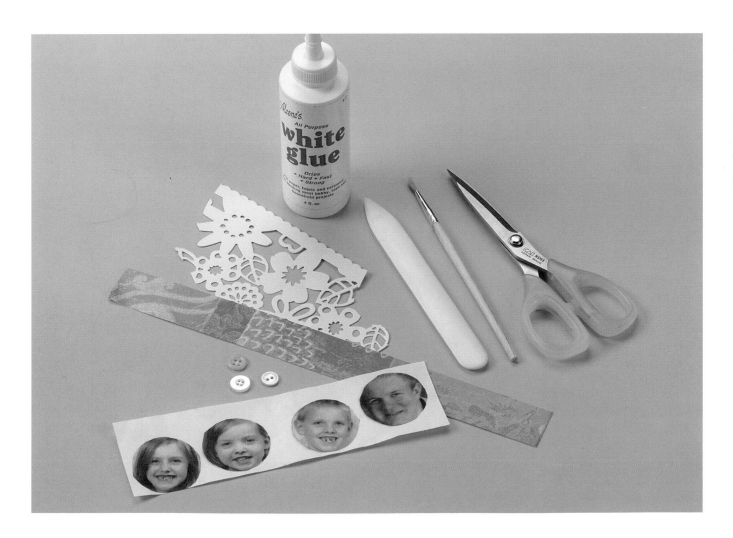

BOOK DOLLS

Book dolls can be journals, a place to record your thoughts, dreams, and inspirations. A book doll could also be used to record an important life event and be treasured as a family heirloom. Often a book doll becomes a gift for a friend. Some book dolls travel from one person to another, with each person adding to the journal, so you want to use durable materials and make a sturdy envelope for the doll's journey.

Pamphlet Stitch

The pamphlet stitch is used to hold the pages to the cover of a book, giving it a professional appearance. It is easy to master and very handy to use on small books.

1 Cut a posterboard cover and fold it in half. Mark the center of the spine.

2 Measure 1½" (3.8 cm) from the center up and down, and mark.

3 Using the awl, make holes for stitching at these three marks.

4 Cut and fold computer paper for the book's pages, to match book cover, but ½" (1.23 cm) smaller all around.

5 Mark and make holes to match cover.

6 With 1 yd. (0.91 m) of thread in the needle, move needle from the outside to the inside at the center hole. Leave at least a 12" (30.5 cm) tail on the outside.

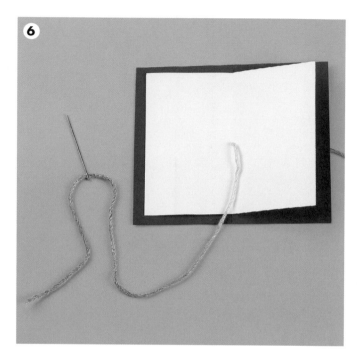

YOU WILL NEED

- posterboard
- 1 yd. (0.91 m) waxed linen or hemp
- large tapestry needle
- awl
- ruler
- blank paper
- five beads

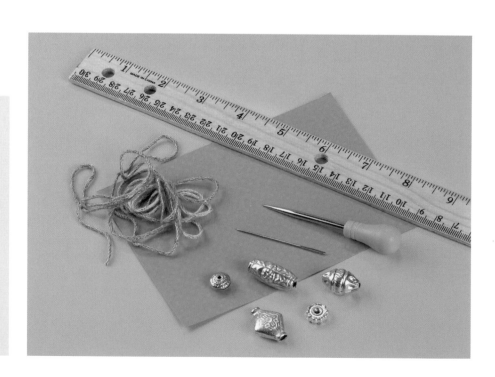

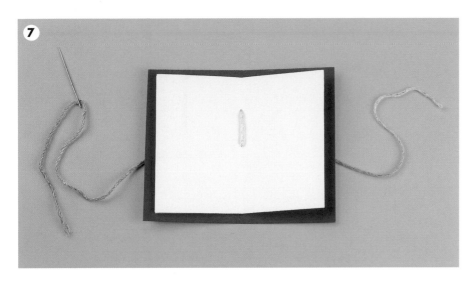

7 Go from the inside to the outside in the top hole and pull tight.

8 Go from the outside to the inside in the bottom hole and pull tight. This creates a long stitch on the outside.

9 Go from the inside to the outside through the center hole, and bring the thread up on the opposite side of the long stitch as the tail. Pull tight and tie a knot over the long stitch with the tails.

10 Slip beads on the threads and knot to hold in place. Trim excess thread.

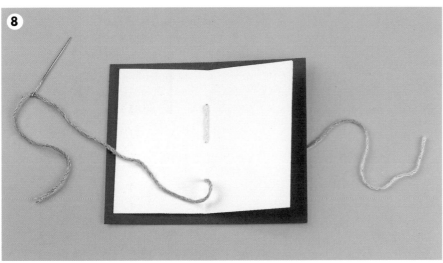

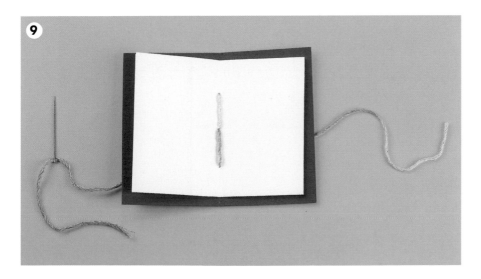

Encaustic Face

YOU WILL NEED

- hot plate
- drawing paper
- crayons
- colored pencils
- eyelash yarn
- glue

Tip

When the plate is hot, the crayons will melt very fast so work quickly.

1 Draw a basic face on the paper using the crayons.

2 Lay the paper on the hot plate. Turn hot plate on to low.

3 With a very light hand, color in the face with the crayons. Colors can be muted by grazing the white crayon over them.

4 Remove paper from the hot plate and let it cool.

5 Draw in details, such as eyelashes, with the colored pencils.

6 Cut around the face allowing a ¼" (6 mm) space from eye level to where the hair will be attached.

Tip

Use a pot holder to lean your hand on while working on the hot plate. Put extra papers below the one you are working on to control heat better.

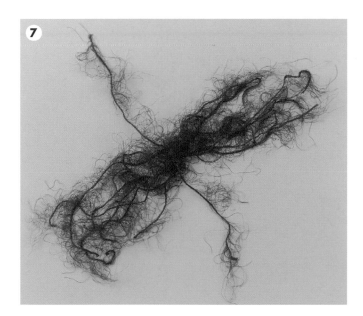

7

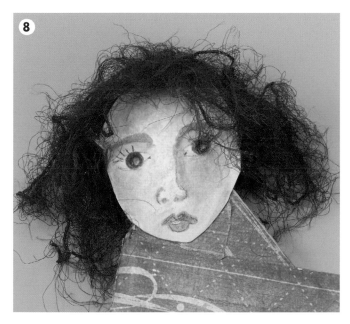

8

7 Cut twelve 7" (17.8 cm) pieces of the eyelash yarn. Lay one piece down and lay the others, perpendicular, over it. Tie piece in a knot holding the other strands together.

8 Glue knot to the top center of the head. Spread glue down the sides of the face and press some of the hair into the glue.

Collage

YOU WILL NEED

- decorative paper
- newspaper
- glue
- glue brush
- posterboard
- wax paper
- bone folder

1 Cut posterboard for the book doll cover. Tear decorative paper into medium-size pieces, trying to minimize the white showing along the tear line.

2 Cover your work area with pieces of newspaper. Using glue and glue brush, apply glue to the back of each piece and arrange the pieces on the cover. Try to use the straight-edged pieces along the edge of the cover.

3 Overlap paper pieces so that every part of the cover is covered.

4 Cover the collage with wax paper, and use the bone folder to press the pieces flat.

Tip

This can be a messy process, so change the newspaper often.

YOU WILL NEED

- 10" x 7½" (25.4 x 19.1 cm) posterboard

- two sheets of decorative paper for collage

- encaustic face 2½" x 2" oval (6.4 x 5.1 cm)

- two plastic hand buttons

- five gold beads

- 1 yd. (0 .91m) gold hemp or waxed linen

- blank paper for pages, 9¼" x 6¾" (23.6 x 17.2 cm)

- large tapestry needle

- awl

- bone folder

- glue

- glue brush

- glue dots

Sunny Day Journal

You can't help but feel upbeat when you jot your thoughts in this cheerful journal. Orange, yellow, and red together make up this Sunny Day Journal.

7 Measure 1½" (3.8 cm) up from the center hole and 1½" (3.8 cm) down from the center hole. Using the awl, make holes in the cover and pages. There will be three holes.

8 Thread the hemp into the tapestry needle and use the pamphlet stitch to bind the pages and the cover.

9 Take the strip of decorative paper reserved in step 1, and fold in half, creating the arms. Fold over 1" (2.5 cm) at each end for cuffs. The arm strip will cover the top of the long stitch, at the spine, and fit just above the center knot. Glue strip in place.

10 Break the shank off of the button hands. Using glue dots, secure hands to the arms at the cuffs.

11 Glue the encaustic face to the top point of the book.

1 Cut a 11" x 1¼" (27.9 x 3.2 cm) piece of the decorative paper to be used as the arms. Set aside.

2 Fold posterboard in half widthwise and crease with the bone folder. This is the spine of the book.

3 Now fold in the top right corner bringing it into the spine fold. Repeat for the left top corner. Crease all folds with the bone folder.

4 The cover (posterboard) will be collaged using the decorative paper.

5 Fold blank paper in the same manner for pages.

6 Mark the center of the blank paper with an awl on the spine crease. Make a hole.

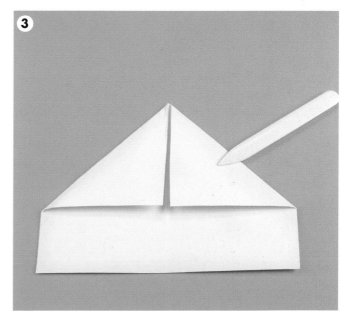

Flat Alice

You will enjoy this flat doll because it can be your companion on a trip and in it you can record your experiences and insert photos. Feel free to embellish her as you wish or make this doll a man or boy. The doll is designed to fit in a mailing envelope and can be used as a round-robin doll where each person mails the doll to a friend and eventually it returns home.

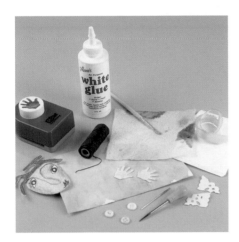

YOU WILL NEED

- hand-painted heavy paper: 4½" x 10¾" (11.4 x 27.3 cm) for body, 1½" x 9¾" (3.8 x 24.8 cm) for arms, and 2" x 2" (5.1 x 5.1 cm) for dress front

- painted paper towel 3" x 4½" (7.6 x 11.4 cm) for apron

- two hands punched from flesh-colored paper

- blank paper for pages of book, 3" x 10½" (7.6 x 26.9 cm)

- waxed linen thread

- large tapestry needle

- two pieces white paper lace

- three small white buttons

- blind portrait face approximately 3" x 3" (7.6 x 7.6 cm)

- blue silk ribbon 12" x ½" (30.5 x 1.3 cm)

- glue and glue brush

- awl

1 Fold the large piece of decorative paper in half widthwise to form doll body.

2 To create the dress, glue the small decorative piece of painted paper in the middle of the body, just above the fold. Glue three buttons and two pieces of paper lace to the dress for an apron.

3 Glue blind portrait face at the top. (See directions for blind portraits on page 91.)

4 Glue a hand at each end of the strip of paper. Wrap the strip around the doll ½" (1.3 cm) above the fold, and glue in the back. Bend arms around to the front of the doll so they face forward when the doll is open. When the doll is closed, the arms go around to keep the doll folded.

5 Find the center of the fold and make a hole with the awl. Make two more holes, 1½" (3.8 cm) from either side of the center.

6 Cut blank pages, fold in half, and make holes at the center of the fold and 1½" (3.8 cm) from the center, to match the holes in the doll body.

7 Thread needle with the waxed linen thread and follow the pamphlet stitch instructions (page 110).

8 Gather paper towel piece on the machine or by hand to fit just above the pages. Glue in place.

9 Glue silk ribbon at the top of the apron and around the back of the doll. Finish with a bow in the center back. Trim the ends.

10 Now Alice is ready for a trip in the mail or with you. She will fit into a 6" x 9" (15.2 x 22.9 cm) manila envelope.

Tips

A small pencil can be attached, on waxed linen thread, around the waist.

The painted paper towel just happens to be the clean-up towel with just a bit more paint added where needed. Paper towels are very sturdy and will work well for many kinds of dolls.

Fabric Journal Doll

Make a fabric doll cover for a journal as a gift or for yourself. Use this basic pattern or construct your own, and design your journal doll to match the creative nature of the words written inside. This project may introduce you to some new ways to use familiar materials. The design of the journal was set up to fit around a notebook purchased at the local art supply store. You may need to adjust the design to fit the notebook you purchase.

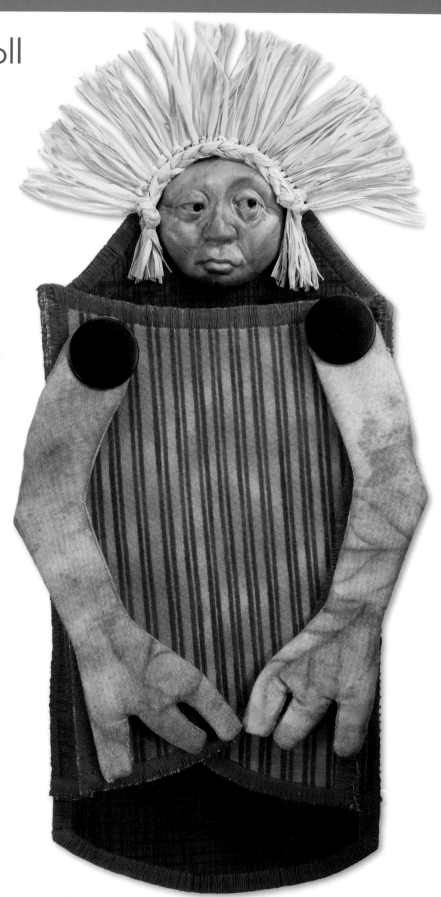

YOU WILL NEED

- three fabric pieces (fat quarters work well)
- felt (white)
- extra-firm stabilizer, such as Peltex
- fusible adhesive, such as Wonder-Under
- two buttons
- clay face
- small notebook, 3" x 5½" x ¾" (7.6 x 14 x 1.9 cm)
- basic sewing supplies
- Fabri-Tac

Tip

You can find Peltex with an adhesive on both sides, so you could omit WonderUnder. However, I like to fuse WonderUnder to Peltex because I feel it makes the book a bit stiffer.

1 Choose which fabric to use for the outside, the inside, and the arms. Iron the fabrics to remove all wrinkles and creases.

2 Cut a piece of stabilizer 15" x 10½" (38.1 x 26.9 cm) and cut two pieces of fusible adhesive the same size. Following manufacturer's instructions, iron a piece of fusible adhesive on each side of the stabilizer. When cooled, remove the paper from both sides.

3 On an ironing board, layer one piece of the ironed fabric wrong side up, the stabilizer, and the other piece of ironed fabric right side up. To prevent the adhesive from sticking to the iron or ironing board, make sure it is completely covered by fabric. Following manufacturer's instructions, fuse fabrics to the stabilizer.

4 Trace the five pattern pieces onto the fabric/stabilizer. (The five pieces are one back, one right side, one left side, and two side flaps.)

5 Cut out the pieces on the pattern lines. Note that the pattern side pieces are the same length but different widths. This will allow for the front flaps of the book to overlap and lay flat.

(continued)

4

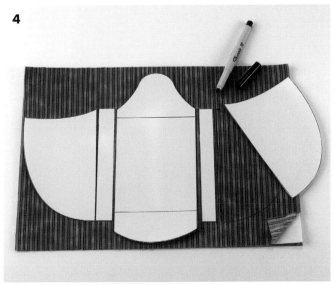

6

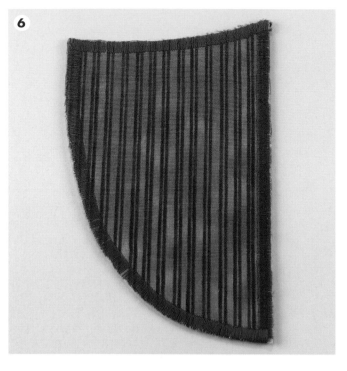

10

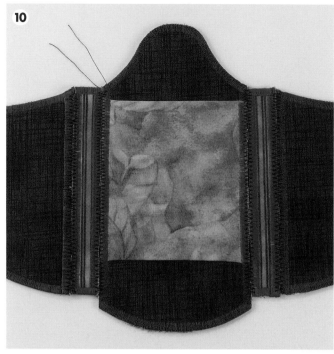

9

6 Stitch a wide and close zigzag stitch around one of the two flap pieces.

7 Sew around the other flap piece and the two sides. Set aside. Do not sew around the back piece yet.

8 To make a sleeve to hold the book in place, cut a 4¼" x 9" (10.8 x 22.9 cm rectangle. We will be using the arm fabric so that the pocket is easier to see and to show how this works. You may wish to use the same fabric as your inside so that the sleeve blends in. Place fabric wrong side up and from the top, fold down a flap 2" (5.1 cm) and up from bottom a flap 2" (5.1 cm).

9 Place this fabric right side up on the back book piece, 2¾" (7 cm) from the top of the back piece. Pin in place and sew with the same zigzag all around the back piece like you did on the other four pieces.

10 Connect the five pieces by stitching between them with a zigzag stitch that is wider than earlier zigzags. This will allow for the pieces to fold over the book and works as a hinge. Black thread was used in the photo for clarity.

11

13

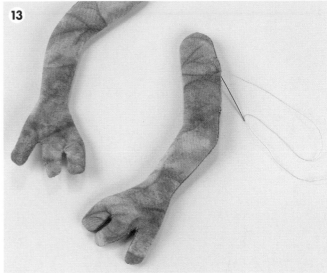

12

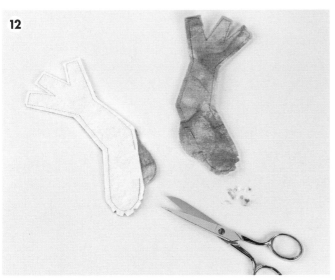

15

11 To make the arms, cut white felt into 6" x 7" (15.2 x 17.8 cm) rectangle. Layer felt, one piece of arm fabric right side up, and second piece of arm fabric wrong side up. The felt gives some volume to the arms without making them stiff. Trace both arms on fabric and mark on back side of arm to leave a 1" (2.5 cm) opening to turn inside out. The traced lines will be your sewing line.

12 Sew around the arms and hands using a close stitch. Carefully cut out and clip curves and corners.

13 Carefully turn and shape the arms and hands. Iron and sew the opening closed.

14 To make your clay face, refer to Tweaked Push Mold Faces (page 136).

15 To finish the Journal Doll cover, sew the arms on the top flap using buttons as embellishments. Glue the face in place with Fabri-Tac and embellish. Slide the back cover of the journal into the sleeve. This is what your Doll Journal looks like open. You can see that we used raffia for hair but you could use lace, yarn, ribbons etc. Have fun and be creative with the design.

CLAY DOLLS

For hundreds of years people have been making dolls of all kinds. Today we make dolls to make us happy, to remember loved ones, even just as toys. The only difference is what we make the dolls out of. In this chapter we will show you how-to make a doll body with a posable wire armature; introduce you to polymer clays and how to use them. Then move on to techniques on how to sculpt a doll head, arms and feet from polymer clay. We will show you how to use push molds and show you ways to tweak them that will never look like a molded face. And as a final project, we'll make a fanciful garden fairy friend with transparent wings.

ARMATURES

The doll body is constructed with armature wire, then covered with quilt batting, and wrapped with strips of T-shirt material. Armature wire is made of aluminum and is lightweight and fully pliable for making sculptures; it is nonstaining and noncorroding. You will find armature wire at your local art supply store. The armature wire used in this book is ⅛" (3 mm). The following instructions are for a cloth-wrapped armature wire body approximately 15" (38.1 cm) without head, hands, and feet.

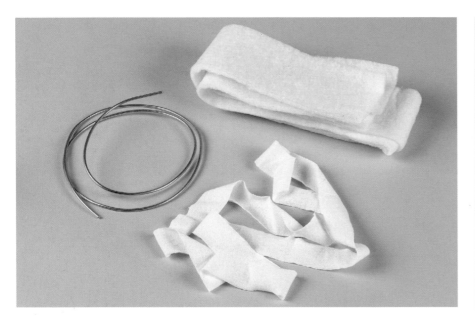

YOU WILL NEED

- armature wire
- quilt batting
- T-shirt, cut into 1" (2.5 cm) strips (cut horizontally across the torso of a T-shirt)
- pliers
- wire cutters
- fast-drying fabric glue, such as Fabri-Tac

1 Cut a piece of armature wire 34" long (86.4 cm); this will become the neck, torso, and legs.

2 Fold this wire in half. Using pliers, twist the folded end to approximately 2" (5.1 cm). This should provide enough length to attach the polymer head when finished.

3 Cut a second piece of armature wire 10" long (25.4 cm) for the arms. Center the wire between the twisted wires and continue twisting wire about 4" (10.2 cm) more. This forms the torso of the doll body.

Tip

You could also try copper wire from you local hardware store. Copper wire is much less flexible but great for larger standing dolls.

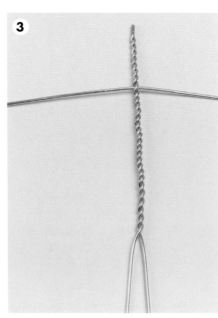

4 To form the hips and legs of the body, bend the wire at a right angle to the torso out 1" (2.5 cm), and straight down, giving your body a stick figure look. Remember that the legs are long and some wire can be removed if your doll is posed sitting.

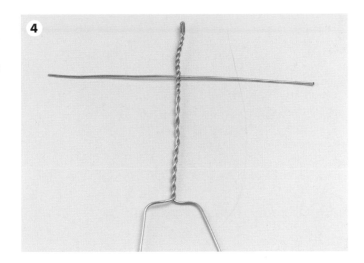

5 Cut a gently worn (or new) T-shirt into 1" (2.5 cm) strips (cut horizontally across the torso of the T-shirt); this will be used to wrap and shape the doll body. You will need many strips of fabric. I suggest cutting the entire torso of the T-shirt.

6 Take a strip of T-shirt and cut the loop; this will give you a long strip of T-shirt. Glue the end to the bottom torso of the wire body using fabric glue.

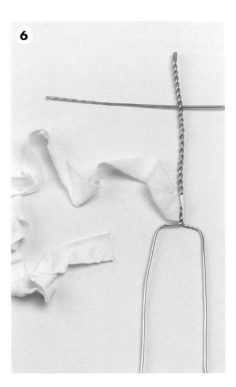

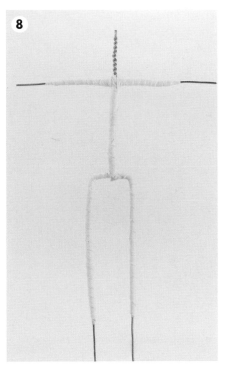

7 Now wrap the T-shirt up the torso, keeping it snug. Wrap out one arm to about 3" (7.6 cm), back to the center, over to the other arm 3" (7.6 cm), and back, then down the torso. If you are using short strips of T-shirt, you may need more than one strip unless it is a large T-shirt. Glue ends of T-shirt with a small amount of fabric glue.

8 Glue another strip to the bottom torso and begin wrapping the legs. Remembering to keep it snug, wrap down to about 7" (17.8 cm), then back up and over to the other leg.

9 Cut the cotton batting into 2" (5.1 cm) strips. Use this to fill out the body (torso) section. You will not need more than 24" (61 cm) or 36"; (91.4 cm) unless you're making a rather plump body.

10 Begin gluing the batting to the bottom of the torso, as you did the T-shirt strips. Go light on the glue. Too much glue will soak through the material and become sticky and hard.

11 Wrap up to the arms and back down again. Make an extra wrap around the lower midsection. If you are planning on a plump doll, wrap the torso several times.

(continued)

Tip

The legs on this will be plenty long and that is done so that if you decide to mount the doll on a base, the wire in the leg can go through the clay foot into a wooden base. This will give extra strength and stability to the doll.

Tip

I only wrap the arms and legs with T-shirt material to get the desired thickness. But when making a plumper doll like a Santa, you may wish to wrap legs with batting to create additional bulk. If you're making a female doll, you may choose to add rolls of batting to the front top for a chest.

12 Make a roll with the batting about 1" x 2" (2.5 x 5.1 cm) and place on the back side of the body for the buttock; glue this on. Then take another piece and glue on top of the buttock and bring to the front like a diaper but up to the arms.

13 Wrap more strips of T-shirt fabric over the batting. This will hold everything in place and firm up the body.

14 Add more thickness to the arms and legs with additional strips of T-shirt. This is what your finished body might look like.

15 Once the arms and feet are made from polymer clay and on the body, you may wish to wrap more T-shirt fabric next to the clay and toward the body. This will give you a smooth transition from clay to the body as well as thicken up arms and legs as they get closer to the body.

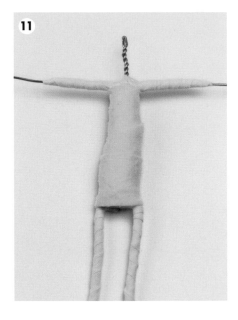

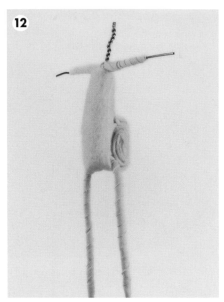

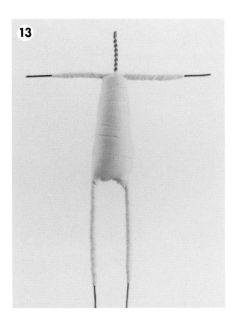

Tip

Use colored strips of T-shirt to function as underwear. I don't always make separate undergarments for dolls but using colored fabric on arms and legs creates the sense of underclothing. (This is a good thing because every doll maker knows that when you display your doll, someone is sure to check to see how it is made and what is under its clothes.)

HOW TO WORK WITH CLAY

Polymer clay is a fun and easy medium. It is amazingly versatile and easy to work with and can be baked in your own home. So with a little practice and patience you will be on your way to creating a head, hands, and feet for your doll. You can find polymer clay at your local art supply store; most will carry two, maybe three kinds, and many more brands can be found online.

Below are a few clays and simple characteristics of each.

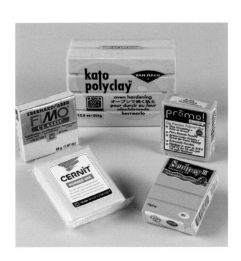

Sculpey: Easy to condition but brittle once baked. Can become very soft when overworked. Available in wide range of colors. Bakes at 275°F (135°C).

Kato Polyclay: Is strong and flexible when baked. Easy to condition and little or no color change when baked, even with repeated bakes. Never sticky or too soft even when over-conditioned. Available in multiple bright colors. Bakes at 300°F (149°C).

Fimo Classic: This clay is stiffer and needs more conditioning. It holds detail well and is strong after baking. Available in multiple bright colors. Bakes at 230°F (110°C).

Premo: Softer and easy to work with right out of the package. Is strong and flexible after baking. This is also a Sculpy product. Bakes at 275°F (135°C).

Cernit: Soft and easy to work with and excellent flesh tones, Cernit clays are strong and very flexible after baking. Bakes at 265°F (129°C).

Each of these clays and other polymer clays will work fine for making your doll parts. Colored clays are widely available and can be combined to create new colors. Many artists mix several brands of clay to combine strength, softness, and flexibility. Each brand of clay may vary slightly in baking temperatures and instructions so read carefully and follow directions to prevent underbaking or burning. The best way to find out what clay you like is to buy a couple kinds of clay and play with it, handle and knead the clay, then bake them and decide what brand you like best.

Here are a few pointers to get you started and help ensure a good experience with polymer clay:

- Clean hands and workspace: This is the key to keeping your clay clean of lint and dirt. You may wish to work on a clean piece of white paper. Many of the polymer clays darken slightly when baked and can hide some lint and dirt. Wearing light-colored clothing can also help.

- Safety: Polymer clay is not meant to be eaten. Keep all clay tools separate from those used for food.

- Conditioning: Warm and knead your clay until smooth and elastic; this makes it easier to work with and sculpt and gives it strength.

- Baking: Be sure to bake at the proper temperature to avoid burning; follow package directions. If needed, test your oven with an oven thermometer for accuracy; bake in the center of oven (toaster oven works well) for even heating. Baking can be done on a piece of paper (a white recipe card works well) or a ceramic tile. Most clays bake at a low temperature and paper will not burn; however, clays should be watched when baking on paper.

This is just a little information to get you started. There is so much more to learn—the best thing to do is to get started and play with some clay!

SCULPTED HEADS

Polymer clay is a great medium for making your doll's head and it's easy to work with when you follow a few simple steps. Clay can give you a very realistic look to the skin with its color and texture, and it is easy enough for children and adults to work with. You may want to clip a few pictures from magazines for references on faces. Let's get started on creating that one-of-a-kind doll head.

YOU WILL NEED

- polymer clay (two packages, approximately 2 oz. [57 g] each)
- two white beads of polymer clay or glass 8 mm
- hand wipes
- aluminum foil
- rolling pin or pasta machine
- knitting needle
- doll needle
- blush
- brush
- knife
- toaster oven

1 Take a square of foil approximately 12" x 12" (30.5 x 30.5 cm) and form into an egg shape. Roll between your hands and on a table surface to smooth. Your foil egg should be approximately 2" tall and ⅝" wide on bottom (5.1 x 1.6 cm) and 1¼" (3.2 cm) wide on top.

2 Condition a block of clay until it is soft and easy to handle, five to ten minutes. Roll the clay between your hands—form it into a ball, rolling into a tube, and folding and rolling again.

3 When clay is easy to work with, flatten it out with a rolling pin or run it through a pasta machine on the largest setting. Roll out clay until it is approximately ⅛" thick (3 mm) and about 5" x 6" (12.7 x 15.2 cm). Put two layers of clay together over the foil and pinch corners; remove excess clay.

4 Continue smoothing clay into the egg shape, removing any dirt, lint, or hair as you go.

Tip

Be careful not to trap air bubbles in the clay. If you see them, use a small needle to let out air and continue conditioning the clay.

Tip

Using the foil helps in three ways. First, it gives you a shape to build your clay from. Second, by having a core of foil, you use less clay. And third, it gives you a more even clay layer to bake, ensuring that the doll head is cured all the way through.

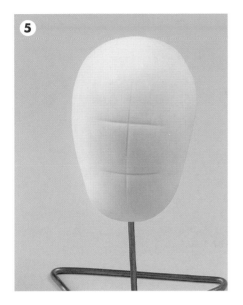

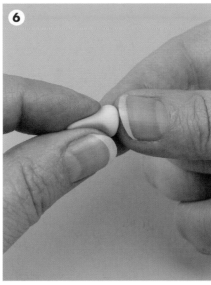

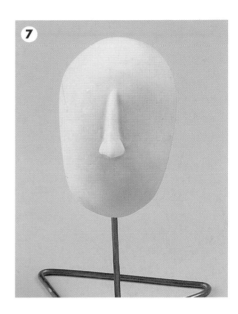

5 With the back of a knife, gently mark the center of the head from left to right. Also divide it into thirds from top to bottom. This divides your working space. The eyes and nose will fit into the center third.

6 To form the nose, condition a small amount of clay into a ball about ⅛" (3 mm) in diameter. Roll into a teardrop shape. Using more clay will give you a larger nose, less equals smaller. Set the teardrop-shaped clay on the index finger of one hand, and use the thumb on the same hand to hold the clay in place. With thumb and index finger of second hand, apply gentle pressure and push down slightly to form a simple nose.

Tip

The eyes should be just under the top line and equal space between eye and nose. Look at them carefully to see that they line up. Look at the face straight on and then turn upside down and look from forehead to chin.

7 Place flat side of nose on the face, and gently blend clay sides to the face. Continue forming nose and smoothing.

8 For the doll's eyes, use white beads made from glass or create your own out of white polymer clay. Roll two round balls approximately ⅜" (1 cm) and bake for ten minutes. Allow to cool.

9 Determine proper placement for the eyes, and then gently push them into the clay face with your thumbs. Make a ⅜" (1 cm) bead from flesh-colored clay and flatten to about ⅛" (3 mm) thick; cut in half. This will make the upper eyelids for each eye. Roll a small cylinder approximately 1/16" (1.6 mm) thick and 1" long (2.5 cm); cut in half. This will form the under eyelid.

(continued)

Tip

If clay gets too soft to work, cool it down for fifteen minutes in the refrigerator.

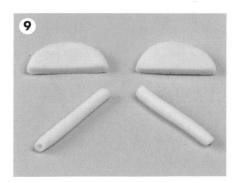

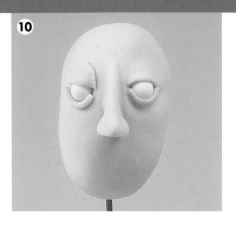

10

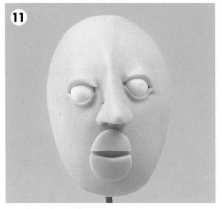

11

12

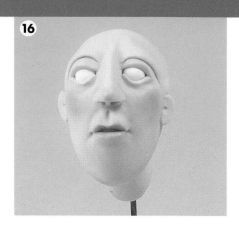

16

10 Position the half circle over the eye, cut edge across the white of the eye. With one piece of the small cylinder, position the rounded end toward the nose and follow the bottom of the eye. Cut off excess clay where the bottom clay cylinder meets the top lid. Gently blend top lids with your fingers and thumb, smoothing the outer edges and leaving a clean straight edge over the eye. Using a knitting needle, blend the bottom lid to the face. Photograph shows placement of clay on left side and clay blended on the right side to how a finished eye might look.

11 To make the mouth, roll a small amount of clay into a ball and flatten to approximately ⅛" (3 mm) thick. Cut in half and place under the nose, leaving a small opening between pieces. This will become the upper and lower lip.

12 Blend the outer edges into the face. To form the bottom lip with a knitting needle, use a rolling motion below the straight edge to form the lip, blending clay into the chin. Round the top lip edges and create a small divot with the knitting needle between the nose and the lips. When the lips are shaped the way you want them, add lines on the lips with a small needle; then gently brush over them with a clean brush.

13 Roll a small amount of clay (pea size) into a cylinder and flatten; cut in two and place on the forehead. This will form the brows. Photograph shows placement on the left and blended clay on the right.

14 To make ears, condition a pea-size amount of clay and flatten to ⅛" (3 mm); cut in half. Place cut edge on side of face and blend only the straight edge to the face; insert small indent with knitting needle, connecting ear to face.

15 For the neck, roll out a cylinder approximately ¾" x 1" (1.9 x 2.5 cm). Give a smooth slight angle cut to both ends and blend clay to head.

16 Before baking the head, check the face to make sure it is smooth and you have not bumped anything. Then with a brush, add blush to the cheeks, tip of nose, and lips. This will bake into the clay. This is what a finished face ready to bake might look like.

17 Bake the head, following manufacturer's directions for temperature and times for baking.

Tip

For easy baking of head, make a small stand out of a short piece of clothes hanger wire. Previous photos were shot on the stand to give you a closer look.

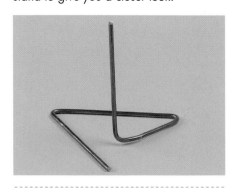

Painting Eyes and Eyebrows

Painting the eyes and eyebrows can really bring your doll's head to life. This technique is easy to do. Just take your time; mistakes are simple to fix. If starting on the face is too much for you, practice the simple steps on paper first.

1

2

3

4

1 When the head has been baked and cooled, it is time to paint the eyes. You only need five colors, we will illustrate with green eyes. Lightly load the liner brush with dark green paint, and paint a circle on the clay eye. I like to connect the top but just almost touch the bottom. Allow paint to dry (five to ten minutes) before starting next step.

2 When the dark paint is dry on both eyes, start the next layer. With the lighter color, paint fine lines from the outside of the eye to the center, sometimes mixing light and dark paint. Go all around the eye, I will often go back and forth between the eyes. This gives the paint time to set up and you won't blend lines that way. Remember not to completely cover up the background color.

3 Add the pupil in the eye using black paint and the back of a small brush or a burnisher/stylus. Dip the handle tip of the brush (or burnisher/stylus) in black and test it on a piece of paper to make sure the size is right. Then place a dot in the center of the painted eye.

4 Add a white highlight in each eye. Make sure that they are both on the same side of each eye. Put them on the top to the side of the pupil.

5 When the paint is dry (I will often leave it overnight), paint lightly over the eye with Fimo varnish. This will brighten the colors and give a wet look to the eyes, making them look more real. Do NOT attempt to use clear fingernail polish. This will yellow the eyes.

6 To create eyebrows, dip a brush in the light brown and, starting to one side of the nose, set the brush and draw an arch. With small faces like this, it's easier to paint an arch rather than many small lines to fill in the eyebrow. Using the same paint, add a few freckles or a beauty mark if desired. You do not need to varnish over eyebrows or freckles.

7 Create hair by gluing natural fibers like sheep or goat hair directly on the clay with fabric glue. Once this is dry, it can be carefully removed in one piece. Depending on the look of the doll, you may want to consider yarns.

Tips

A craft knife can easily clean up small mistakes. Gently scrape off paint that you don't want. If you have made a major mistake, gently wash the paint off, dry, and start over.

When painting the iris, I often hold the head upside down. The face is less distracting, and I can concentrate on just painting two circles.

SCULPTED HANDS AND FEET

Now that you have completed your polymer clay head, hands and feet will be easier. The more you use polymer clay, the better you get. Remember to think about what your doll is going to be doing—is it sitting, standing, holding, or pointing to something? Whatever you choose, let the hands and feet tell the story.

YOU WILL NEED

- Polymer clay (one package approximately 2 oz. [57 g])
- hand wipes
- knitting needle
- doll needle
- blush
- brush
- knife
- toaster oven

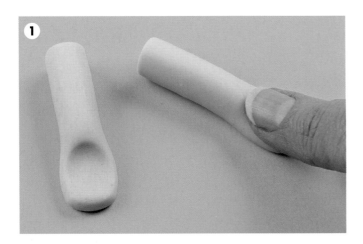

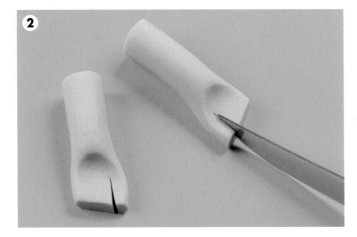

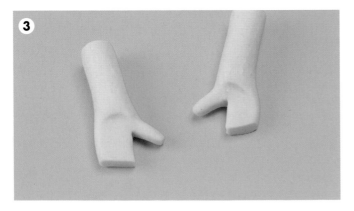

Sculpting Hands

1 Condition the clay until it is soft and easy to handle, three to five minutes. Roll the clay between your hands and form into a ball; roll out into a cylinder to approximately 4½" long x ½" thick (11.4 x 1.3 cm). Cut in half, and with your thumb press down on one end of each cylinder approximately ¾" (1.9 cm) long. This will form the palm of each hand.

2 Set the two paddle-shaped pieces side by side and cut at a slight angle across the top of the depressed clay. Next, cut each hand as shown; this will become the thumb.

3 To shape thumb, gently bend the clay out and, using your thumb and fingers, smooth and shape it. A gentle rolling back and forth works well for this.

4 Form fingers by rolling out a long cylinder approximately 5" long x ⅛" thick (12.7 cm x 3 mm). Cut into four pieces and gently round one end of each finger by rolling clay tips between your thumb and first finger. Set the pieces in a row, stepping fingers like your real hand. The first and third finger should be about the same length, the pinky shorter, and the second finger the longest. Cut bottom at an angle to match palm and fit on the hand.

Tip

Work on both clay hands at the same time, you have a better chance of ending up with a right and left hand.

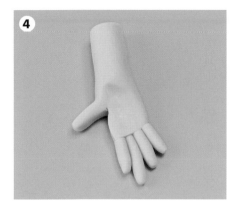

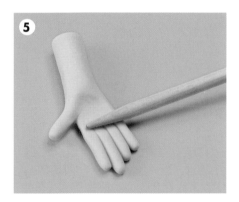

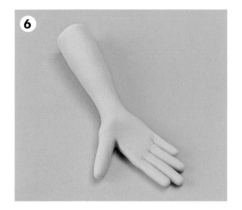

5 Gently blend fingers to hand using your fingers and a knitting needle. Use the heat of your hands to soften the clay and take your time, using light, gentle strokes.

6 To form a wrist, place the polymer hand (just below its thumb) between your thumb of one hand and first finger of the other and gently rotate. This will narrow the clay into a wrist shape.

7 Add lines to the hands to help form dimension and character. For reference, look at your own hands and compare shape and lines. Insert a short length of armature wire into each hand before baking, so they can be removed and placed on your armature body's arms.

Tip

If you would like to have the doll's hands hold or gesture something, now is the time to do it. Let's say you want your person to hold a crystal ball (a clear marble is perfect and can be baked), form the hand around it and bake it. Remember that not everything can withstand baking in an oven without melting.

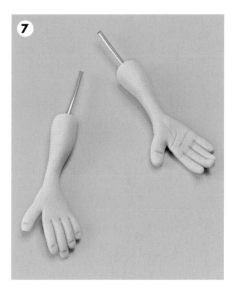

Tips

A flat curved end of a cuticle stick is a perfect tool for making indents for fingernails.

Before baking, check that everything is smooth and shaped the way you want. Once the clay is baked, it stays in that shape.

Remember to read and follow the baking directions for the type of clay you choose. I generally bake clay in a heated oven (toaster ovens works great) on a piece of paper for twenty to thirty minutes, then turn off the oven and allow the clay to cool in oven. If you are afraid that you will forget the baked pieces in the oven, remove them and handle them as little as possible until cool.

Tip

The length of the fingers can vary. If you want every thing to be proportionate, a hand and fingers would be similar to the length of the face from chin to hairline. Otherwise be creative.

Sculpting Feet

1 Condition the clay until soft and easy to handle, three to five minutes. Roll the clay between your hands and form into a ball. Begin rolling out into a cylinder, about 4½" long x ½" thick (11.4 x 1.3 cm). Cut in half, so you have two 2¼" long x ½" (5.7 x 1.3 cm) pieces. Bend the bottom 1" (2.5 cm) to form the foot, giving you an "L" shape.

2 Shape the foot by applying light pressure with your hands. Gently stroke and rub the clay to smooth and shape it. Working on both feet at the same time will help ensure that you have a right and left foot and that the sizes are similar. At this point, the foot should be wedge-shaped.

Tip

If you need a reference to what feet look like, take your shoes off.

3 To form the heel, hold the clay foot between your thumb and first fingers, and with your thumbs gently smooth clay to form and shape the heel. Gentle strokes and heat from you fingers will move and shape the clay easily.

4 To create toes, use a needle or the back of a knife to gently mark the placement of toes. Remember to count, and size the toes appropriately. Cut the clay, dividing the clay toes.

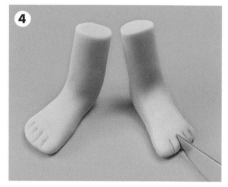

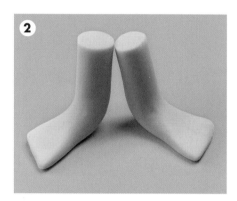

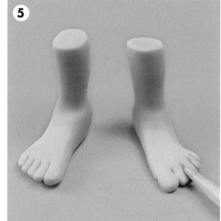

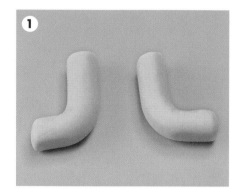

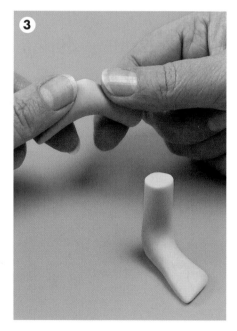

5 Taking your time, round and shape the toes with your fingers and the knitting needle. You can gently pull toes out of place and rock clay back and forth to round sides and end then gently put them back in place.

6 To finish the feet, taper the ankles and add lines under the foot. Bake with armature wire in place.

7 When hands and feet have been baked and cooled, place them on the wrapped armature body. This is what all your parts assembled might look like.

8 This is what a dressed doll can look like. Meet "Fin."

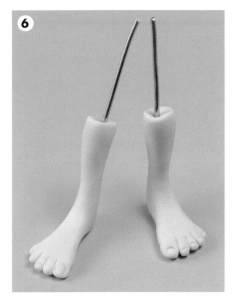

6

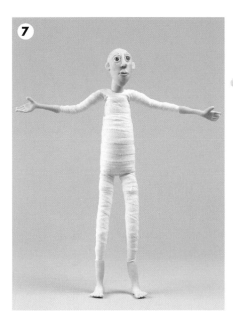

7

8

Tip

If you're going to have shoes on your doll, shape the foot and don't divide the toes. This will help create more realistic shoes and unless you have open-toe shoes, the toes will not be visible.

TWEAKED PUSH MOLD FACES

Push mold faces are a quick and easy way to create a face for a doll. If creating your own head is more work than you are up to, then this is an easy alternative. Check your local art or craft store or even online for a variety of faces. With these techniques, you can easily create a face and change it so no two will look the same.

YOU WILL NEED

- push mold
- clay
- brush
- cornstarch
- beads
- artist chalks
- toilet paper
- watercolors
- knitting needle
- knife
- ripple cutter

How to Use a Push Mold

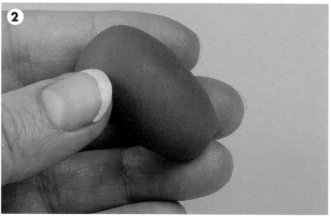

1 When working with polymer clay, wash and clean your workspace and hands well to help keep clays clean and free of lint. Now brush your push mold with cornstarch (this will keep clay from sticking to the mold), turn mold upside down, and tap lightly to remove excess cornstarch.

2 Condition polymer clay in to smooth cone shape, estimating the amount needed to fill the mold.

3a

Tip

If you have difficulty removing the clay, condition another small piece of polymer clay and press into the back of the molded piece. Then gently pull the clay out of the mold.

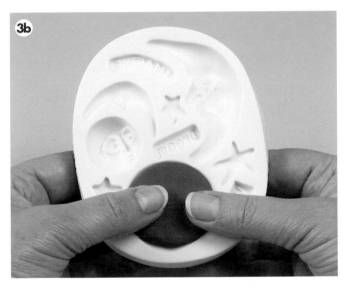

3b

5

3 Place the point of the polymer clay into the center of the mold. Press the clay to fill the mold.

4 Bend the mold slightly and gently remove the polymer clay.

5 Set the molded clay on paper. It is ready for tweaking.

Tip

If you use too much clay, you can remove the excess with a flat knife across the top when the mold is still in place.

Tweaking Faces

Get creative and tweak some push mold faces by stretching, pinching, cutting, pushing, or compressing the molded faces into different shapes. You can even color them. If you don't like what you have created, simply recondition the clay and try again. The photos on pages 138 and 139 offer ideas for tweaking your push mold face.

(continued)

1 To stretch the molded face, gently pull and pinch off clay all the way around the face. Shown is original face and stretched. For this face we used Kato clay, copper color, and set beads into eyes. Baked at 300°F (149°C) for thirty minutes.

2 To cut a molded face, simply cut the face apart with a knife. You can see that we used a rippled cutter on this face. We used gold Premo clay and set beads into eyes. Baked at 275°F (135°C) for thirty minutes.

3 Push or compress the molded face by pushing in from all sides to condense or to make the face smaller. We used red Fimo clay and set beads into eyes. Baked at 230°F (110°C).

4 Color the baked face with artist chalks. Color on baked face with chalks, blend with fingers, and polish with a paper towel. We used flesh Fimo clay. Baked at 230°F (110°C).

Tips

Try cutting faces from different clays and putting them back together for a Picasso look.

5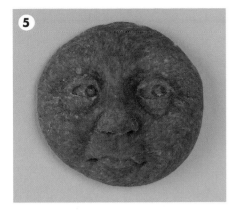

6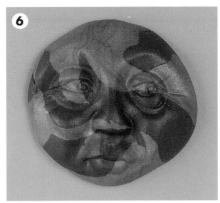

For something really different, wet toilet paper slightly and press it into the mold with a small brush. Add layers one at a time until the mold is filled. To color the face, dip the brush in watercolor before tamping each layer in place. Allow the paper to set in the mold overnight; then remove the face to finish drying. The finished face will look like it is made of handmade paper.

5 Try using premixed clay to get a different look. Here you can see we used a mixed clay to give a bark look to the face. You can buy other mixed clays that look like this or stone and come in a variety of colors. We used Fimo clay baked at 230°F (110°C).

6 Try combining two colors but not completely to give a mottled look. For this face we took two small amounts of polymer clay and conditioned separately, rolled into small snakes, twisted together, then rolled into a cone. We used Premo gold and Kato copper. Baked at 275°F (135°C).

7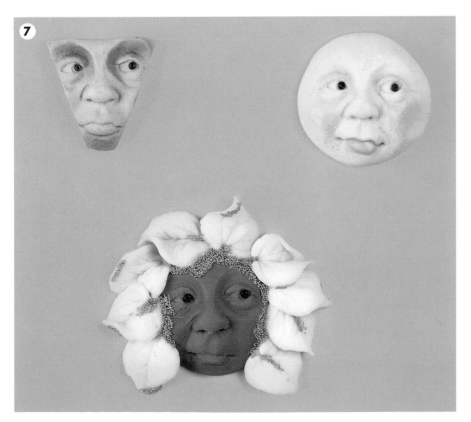

7 Try baking a face and, when cooled, paint with acrylic paint and wipe off right away for a stained look. Add beads, brush-on glitter, or blush before baking. Enhance face details with a knitting needle. Apply powders to unbaked face, then bake. What you can do with the face is only limited by what you think of. You can even grind up crayons in small pieces and mix in clay before baking.

Garden Fairy

Garden fairies are a fun and whimsical project for all year round. You will learn basic skills to make your fairy's head, hands, and feet out of polymer clay with a wire body and transparent wings. Dress it up with flower petals and felt for clothing. Then hang it with fishing line, and you will truly think it is flying.

1 Cut a 12" (30.5 cm) piece of armature wire for the torso and a 4" (10.2 cm) piece of wire for the arms. Fold the 12" (30.5 cm) piece in half. Using the pliers, twist the folded end to about ½" (1.3 cm). This will become the fairy's neck.

2 Center the 4" (10.2 cm) wire between wires under the neck. Continue twisting torso wire until twisted about 2½" (6.4 cm) from the top fold. This stick figure forms the armature for the fairy body.

3 Wipe oils from the armature wire with a hand wipe. This will help keep the polymer clay clean. Set the armature aside. Clean your work space and tools well to keep dirt and lint out of the clay.

(continued)

YOU WILL NEED

- one package polymer clay, about 1.97 oz (56 g)
- 2 yd (1.83 m) bias cut ribbon
- flesh-colored or lighter yarn
- two small glass seed beads (9/0 Czech seed beads)
- 1" (2.5 cm) clay pot
- Angelina film for wings
- 26-gauge wire
- white craft glue
- blush
- armature wire (can be found at your local art material store)
- flower petals
- felt

- fast-drying fabric glue, such as Fabri-Tac
- fish line
- hand wipes
- knitting needle
- doll needle
- small brush
- pressing paper
- candle
- two pliers
- knife
- basic sewing supplies
- wire cutters
- paper and pencil
- transparent tape
- tweezers
- toaster oven

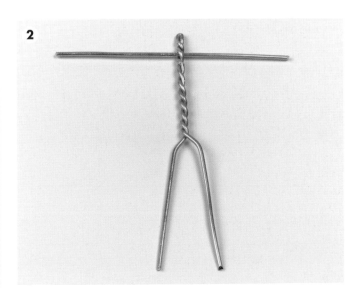

1

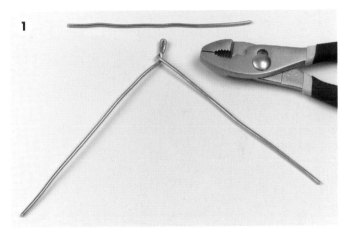

2

4 Divide the clay into thirds with your knife: ⅓ for arms and feet, another ⅓ for torso, and ½ of the last ⅓ for head. The extra clay may be used for the nose, ears, and to give more shape to the torso.

5 Take the first ⅓ of the clay and condition until soft and easy to handle, three to five minutes. Roll the clay between your hands and form into a ball. Begin rolling into a cylinder approximately ⅜" (1 cm) thick and 7¾ to 8" (19.7 to 20.3 cm) long. Cut in two.

6 To make hands and forearms, bend one of the cylinders into a U shape. This will help ensure that you end up with a right and left arm/hand.

7 To form the palm side of the hands, use your thumb to press down both ends of the cylinder approximately ½" (1.3 cm).

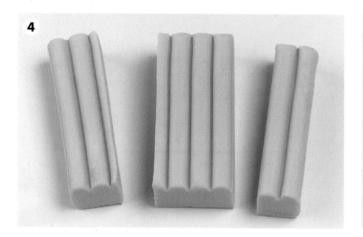

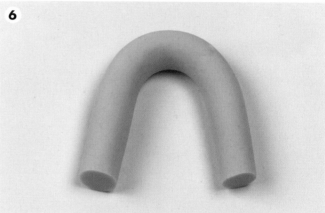

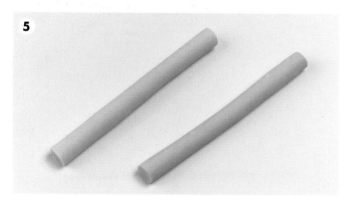

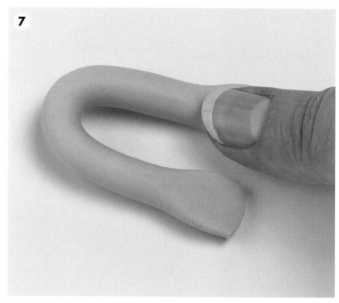

Tip

If clay is very stiff, place in clean baggy and hold under your armpit to warm and soften for five to ten minutes. To keep the clay that you're not currently working with warm, put it into a bag and sit on it.

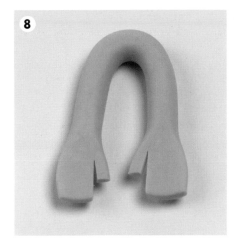

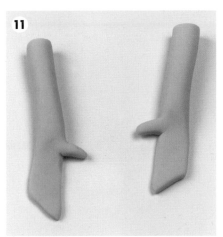

8 Using the knife, cut inside of both palms approximately ⅛" (3 mm) wide. This will become the thumb. Cut top of thumb down approximately ⅟₁₆" (1.6 mm) from top.

9 Begin creating thumb by bending to center; use your thumb and first finger to blend edges away and form thumb.

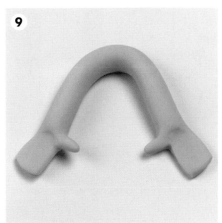

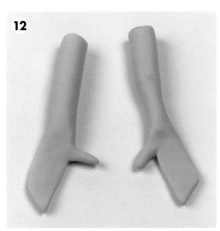

10 To form the hand, begin softening the two sides and top with your fingers, or use a knitting needle by rolling along edge. Elongate the clay and bring to a slight point.

11 Cut clay, dividing it into two arms and hands. Straighten cut ends.

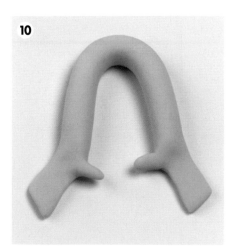

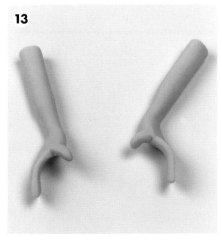

12 Roll the clay just below hand between your thumb and first finger to form wrist. Don't roll out too narrow or this will be come a weak point.

13 Bend the hand back and shape the hand and thumb to give them character.

(continued)

Tip

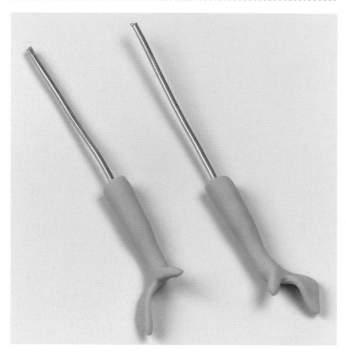

Twist the wire with a drilling motion to insert into the clay. Insert the wire only up to the wrist and avoid poking through the clay.

Tip

If you don't have time to finish your fairy in one setting, you can bake it in sections. Just make sure you bake them with a piece of wire armature in them.

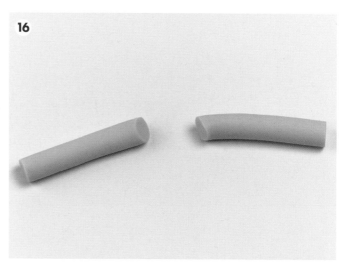

16

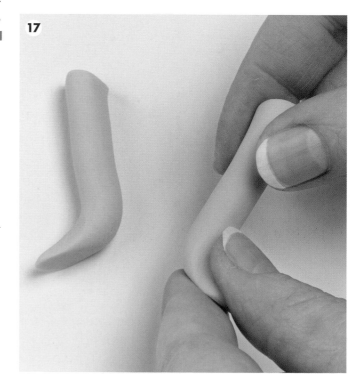

17

14 The arms will need to go over the armature wire, so take a doll needle and carefully poke in the cut end (elbow) of clay; then take a short piece of armature wire and insert it into the arm.

15 Make sure the arms are smooth and shaped the way you want them. You may need to trim the ends of both arms to make the same length. Set aside.

16 To make the lower leg and feet, take the other clay cylinder that you already rolled and cut it in half, making two short cylinders approximately 4" long (10.2 cm).

17 Bend the end of each cylinder about ¾" (1.9 cm) to begin forming the foot. To form the heel, gently rub and pat the clay into a heel bulge. Smooth the top and bring toes to a point.

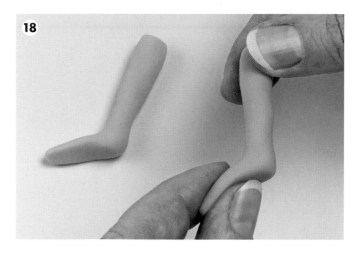

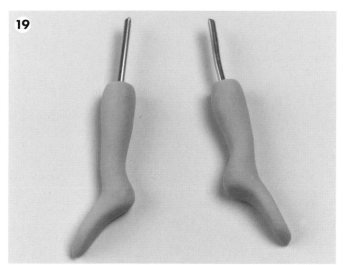

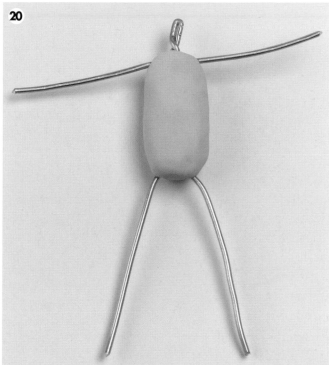

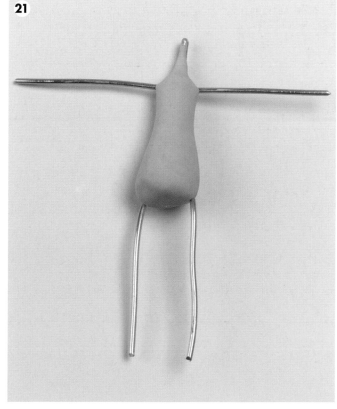

18 Give the foot a little more character by pressing your thumb on the inside of each foot to form an arch.

19 Finish by shaping toes and slightly point the foot similar to that of a ballerina. This will help create the illusion that the garden fairy is flying and not just standing in the air. Use the doll needle to start holes in each leg and insert armature wire in leg for baking.

20 To begin working on the fairy torso, take the next ⅓ clay and condition it well. Roll a ball in your palms and make it into an oval. Cut clay in half from top to bottom, and place on front and back of the stick figure armature.

21 Blend sides together, gently shaping torso. Bring a little clay up from the shoulders to form a neck. Set body aside.

(continued)

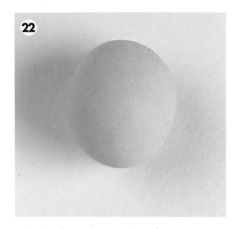

22

Tip

For beginners, it may be easiest to place the clay head on the end of your knitting needle. Inserting the knitting needle at the angle the head would be attached to the neck. This will allow you to work on the fairie's head without holding onto the clay, keeping it smooth and round.

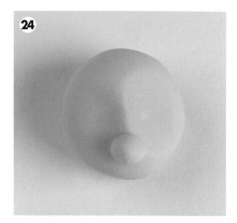

24

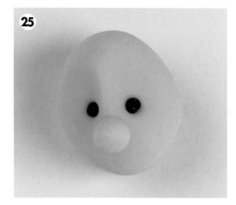

25

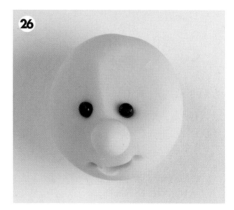

26

23

23 Once you have the right size, hold the clay ball between your fingers and gently press both thumbs into the clay, shaping the upper portion of clay for eyes and nose. Gently smooth the head to get rid of bumps and fingerprints.

24 For the nose, condition a small amount of clay into a ball approximately ⅛" (3 mm), smaller or larger as desired. Gently push it onto the face and shape.

25 Place one glass seed bead on a needle and position above and to the side of the nose. Do the same for the other side.

26 Create a mouth by drawing a smile with the tip of the knife blade. Deepen it with the blade and work it open. Add fairy dimples at each corner of the mouth using a blunt needle or stylus.

22 To form the head, take half of the clay that is left and condition. Roll into ball approximately ¾" (1.9 cm); check to see if the size is in scale with the body. If it is a little small, add some clay; if it's too large, remove some.

Tip

Black beads work well for eyes but don't be afraid to try colored beads or small crystals.

27 For ears, condition a small amount of clay and make a ball about ¼" (6 mm), gently flattening while making it into an oval.

28 Cut the oval in half, making right and left sides. Bring the smaller end of clay to a point by applying light pressure with your finger and thumb; smooth out. Roll your finger on the bottom to round it off, making the lobe part of the ear.

29 Place ears on each side of the face and check placement to see if they are even. Press the front part to the head, and blend into the face with your knitting needle. Leave a point at the top and an earlobe at the bottom. Make a small dimple in each ear using the blunt needle.

30 Remove fairy head from the knitting needle and place on the body. Check that the face and body are as smooth as you would like. If not, take a brush and gently smooth off fingerprints.

(continued)

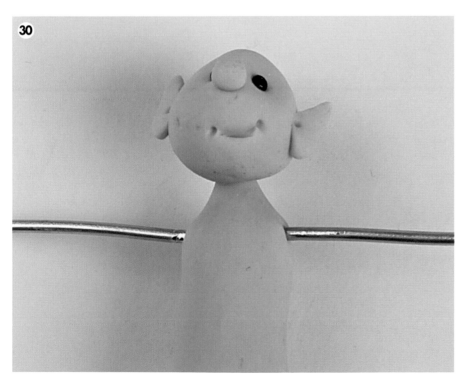

Tip

I use a ⅜" (1 cm) angle shaped brush to remove fingerprints. Remember to keep the brush clean and you will keep your clay clean.

Tip

If you are unsure about your oven temperature, purchase a small oven thermometer. This will ensure proper baking temperature and strength of clay.

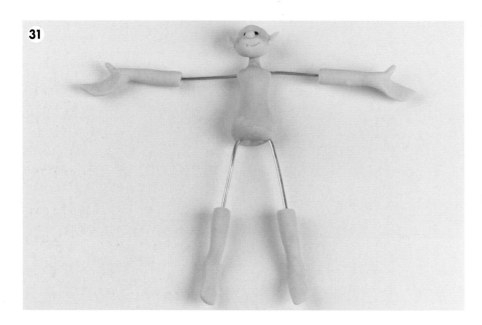

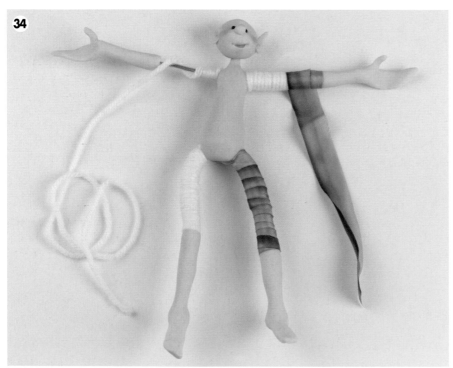

31 Before baking, add a little blush on the cheeks, nose, chin if desired. Go light on this, as you can always add more color. The clay color will darken as it bakes and the blush will seem to lighten in color. Use a tapestry needle to place a hole in the fairy's back for wings.

32 Put the arms and legs on the wire. Make sure the legs and arms are on well and place on a piece of cardstock, such as a 4" x 6" (10.2 x 15.2 cm) recipe card. Pre-heat toaster oven, according to directions on polymer clay package. Bake the fairy; then allow to completely cool. (The clay is fragile and flexible in a warm state.)

33 Fill in the area between the arms and body as well as the body and legs by wrapping yarn around the armature wire. Begin by gluing yarn to the wire with fabric glue. Allow glue to set up (three to five minutes); then begin wrapping the yarn around the wire. Keeping the yarn snug as you can, move down to the clay arm and back until the arm appears solid. Glue the end of the yarn. Repeat with the other arm and legs.

34 Put a small dot of fabric glue on the leg, and place the ribbon on the glue. Wrap ribbon around the leg until you reach the body. Glue the ribbon end to the back side of body. If you plan the wrapping right, you can use the ribbon as part of the clothing. Set the fairy aside.

35 Copy wing patterns on page 203. The lines indicate placement for wire. We have drawn the wings with a top and bottom wing and given both sides so that you can work on all wings at once.

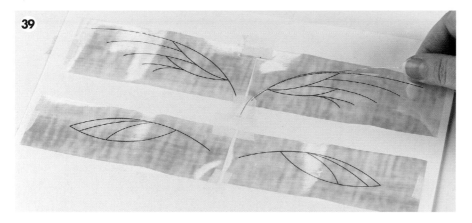

39

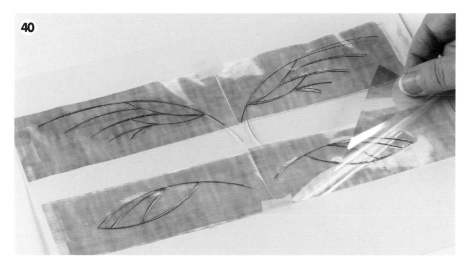

40

Tip

Wings add a lot of expression to the fairy. You can create wings with more detail, such as curls of wire, glitter, and even beads.

36 Lay the film over the wing design and secure it at each end with tape. Cut the film into four parts before placing it on the design. This makes it easier to handle and wastes less film. Taping the film gives you a flat working space to glue the wires to.

37 Unroll about 2' (61 cm) of wire and cut. Place one end on the tip of the wing design and follow the shape of the wing; cut the wire to length. Do the same for each wing, cutting and shaping a wire for each line.

Tips

The size of the wings is determined by the size of the film. Most Angelina film comes 4" (10.2 cm) wide so make your wings fit the film. If you want larger wings, make multiple pieces and combine them.

To keep the film free of excess glue, use a tweezers to run wire through glue and place wires on the wing design.

Don't worry if the glue smears. Once it is dry and the wings are ironed, the glue will not show. If you get a large drop on the film, it is best to remove it with hand wipes or a cotton swab.

38 Apply a line of glue to a 4" x 4" (10.2 x 10.2 cm) square of paper. Run the wire across the glue in a smooth, sweeping motion. Do not cover the entire wire in glue; you only need to coat the side placed on the film.

39 Carefully place the wire over the wing design and onto the film. The first and longest piece may need to be held in place until the glue holds.

40 Continue gluing the wires onto the film, following your drawn design. Then, cut another set of film to place on top of the wires. Set the wings aside and place a book on top to hold wires and film together. Leave this overnight or until glue is no longer white but clear.

41 Carefully remove the tape from the design and film. Once the wire and film are free from the paper design, prepare to iron the wings.

(continued)

Tip

Tip

Be careful when setting your iron temperature. Too much heat will melt the wings. You can always turn up the heat on the iron if needed.

42 Warm up the iron to a medium heat or silk setting. Place a wing between pressing paper and move iron over the wing for a few seconds. The film will bond to itself and change color slightly when ironed. Finish ironing the rest of the wing parts.

43 Trim excess film from the wings, leaving approximately ⅛" (3 mm). The film that's left will be melted and form a sealed edge around the wing.

44 To melt the excess film, light a candle and hold the edges of the wing up to the flame. Move the wing slowly and watch the film melt up to the wire. Go all around the wing and melt scallops on the open end of the larger wings.

45 Layer the two largest wings next to each other, then the smaller wings on either side. Twist the end wires together.

Make a small wire loop for hanging. Twist it together with the wing wires. The twisted wire will be inserted into the fairy's back to hold up the wings. Trim wire to ¼" (6 mm) long, and check that it will fit into the fairy's back.

46 To finish dressing the fairy, attach large flower petals for a skirt, smaller petals for hair, and a small flower pot for a hat. Create a jacket (see pattern on page 204) out of felt with bead buttons. Hand-sew the jacket to the fairy. Cut a small V-shape in the back to allow the wings to be glued to the fairy's back.

47 Cut 1 yd. (0.91 m) of fish line, run one end through the hanging loop, and tie the two ends together. Hang the fish line on a hook. Bend the fairy's arms and legs, and open the wings.

Variations

Make fairies for all holidays and
seasons by using traditional colors
and themes. Halloween fairies, fall
fairies, Christmas fairies . . . the
ideas are endless!

CLOTH ART DOLLS

Many art dolls are made from fabric with fiberfill stuffing. Their body shapes can suggest movement and emotions, or they can be very abstract. There are various ways to make faces for cloth art dolls, so you can give them expressions. The fabrics you choose also influence the final outcome, since color plays a large part in the perception of any art object. Once you learn the techniques for making these dolls, feel free to experiment with combining them to make unique art dolls of your own.

CLAY FACES AND HANDS

You can make expressive faces and hands for cloth dolls using polymer clay. Follow the instructions on pages 135 to 140 for working with polymer clay. With the methods that follow, you can make faces and hands that can easily be attached to the stuffed cloth bodies of art dolls. A doll face doesn't have to look like a real person. This clay face is easy to make and you don't have to be an artist to get good results. As you experiment with different faces, you will develop your own style.

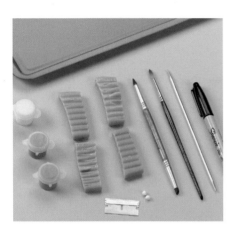

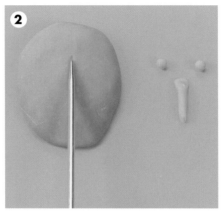

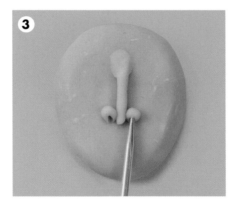

YOU WILL NEED

- flesh-colored polymer clay
- small amount of white polymer clay
- clay shaper tool
- double-pointed knitting needle
- fine-tipped watercolor brush
- single-edged razor blade
- old pie pan or cookie sheet
- acrylic paint: red tones, white, purple or green
- medium-tip and fine-tip black markers
- straight pin
- oven

Clay Faces

1 Roll a piece of flesh-colored softened clay into a ball the size of a small plum. Press down with the palm of the hand on a flat surface and form a cabochon-style piece. The bottom will be flat and the top domed. Measure to see that the face is the right size for the doll you wish to make.

2 Shape the face piece in an oval and mark the nose position by making a groove with the knitting needle.

3 Make the nose pieces by rolling clay into a thin snake shape and hold it up to the face to see if it is the correct size (about 1¼" long [3.2 cm]). Cut with the razor blade and press down at one end to flatten. Put the nose in the groove and work the flattened end into the forehead with the clay shaper or needle. It works best to roll the side of the tool against the clay. Now cut two pieces from the snake and work them into equal sized balls. These will fit next to the nose to form nostrils. To make the hole in the nostril, poke a hole with the knitting needle, and press down.

4 With the clay shaper, make two impressions on either side of the nose for the eye sockets.

5 Make two small balls of white clay for the eyeballs. Press the balls lightly into the eye sockets.

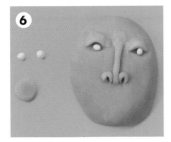

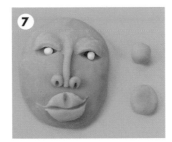

10 Smear a small amount of red paint on the cheeks and wipe off to get the blush look desired. Paint the lips red with the small paintbrush. Use the small brush to paint on eye shadow and smudge, if desired. When paint is dry, use the medium-tip black marker to make eyes. Dip a straight pin into the white paint and make the white gleam in each eye. Use the fine-tip black marker to make eyelashes.

Clay Hands

Hardened polymer hands can be purchased in a few sizes but there are a couple of different ways to make your own. You can use "cookie cutters" specially made for making hands. Or you can form the clay arms and hands freeform from coils of clay, giving them their own unique shape.

Cookie-Cutter Hands

1 Pat or roll out well-conditioned polymer clay and cut out hands with the cutter.

2 Place hands on a cookie sheet. Bake accordingly.

Freeform Hands

1 Condition clay and roll into small snake shapes.

2 Form snakes into hand shapes. Look at your own hand for a guide. A razor blade is the easiest way to cut fingers to the right length. Press down and smooth the palm area. Place on cookie sheet or pan and bake.

6 Form a small piece of flesh-colored clay into a ball the size of a blueberry and flatten it. Cut in half to form two eyelids. Bend pieces a bit and lay the lids partway over the eyeballs. Using the clay shaper, smooth the edges along the nose, forehead, and edge of face.

7 Make a small ball of clay and flatten for lips. Test to see if the size is right for the mouth. With the knitting needle, make a groove to separate top from bottom lips. With clay shaper make the groove in the top lip.

8 Before baking, make three holes in the top of the face for stitching to the body. (These can be drilled, if necessary.)

9 When the face is completely assembled, place on an old pie pan or cookie sheet and bake, following manufacturer's instructions. Allow the face to cool before handling.

Tips

Set the oven temperature according to the instructions on the clay wrapper. Make sure you are baking at the correct temperature for your oven. Watch the time specified carefully. Clay can darken if cooked too long or at too high a temperature. Make sure to ventilate the kitchen while clay bakes.

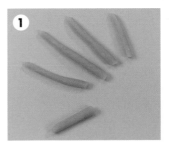

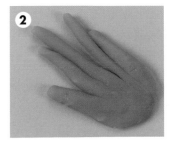

Art Doll with Clay Face I

The body shape for this doll is very simple, so the fabric you choose and the embellishments you add will give your doll its character. She stands about 13" (33 cm) high. Embroidery and beading accent her arms and she wears a necklace with a charm that helps describe her nature. Her dread locks were fashioned from thick-and-thin yarn.

YOU WILL NEED

- ½ yd. (0.46 m) printed cotton fabric
- fiberfill
- one clay face, 3½" (8.9 cm) long
- one clay hand
- sharp tapestry needle
- purple perle cotton
- multicolor thick-and-thin yarn
- purple seed beads
- black beading thread
- beading needle
- necklace: silver bracelet chain, 9" (22.9 cm), silver dragonfly charm
- basic sewing supplies
- white craft glue
- weight bag
- hemostat

1 Enlarge the pattern (page 204) 200%, and cut it out. Fold fabric and cut two body pieces, using pattern as a guide. Cut two arm pieces.

2 With right sides facing, stitch body pieces together with a ½" (1.3 cm) seam, leaving an opening at the bottom.

3 Turn right side out and stuff with fiberfill. Insert a weight bag in the bottom to help the doll stand. Finish stuffing.

4 Turn under ½" (1.3 cm) along the bottom edge and slip-stitch closed. Turn the pointed ends toward the center and stitch in place.

5 Pin the arm pieces on the body, with the long straight sides along the side seams. Using a running stitch (page 180), attach arms to body with regular thread, leaving the cuff edges open.

6 Stitch around the arms with the perle cotton in a chain stitch, leaving the cuff edge open. This stitching will cover the raw edge of the arm and also the thread.

7 Stuff the arms with fiberfill using the hemostat.

8 Decorate the cuff edge with a beaded fringe. Using the beading needle and thread, attach to cuff edge, add eight beads and then back through the last seven beads. The eighth bead is the turn bead. Pull up firmly and make a stitch in the fabric. Continue up the edge and then add more fringe to fill in on the way back down. Knot off.

9 Glue both sides of the bottom edge of the hand and push into the arm hole.

10 Attach the clay face to the head with beading thread through the three holes at the top of the head.

11 To create the hair, cut the thick-and-thin yarn so that each piece has a thin area and a thick area. Sometimes different lengths are needed so the thick end will be cut to make pieces shorter.

12 Place glue on the thick end of the yarn and arrange the hair on the doll. Make sure you cover the holes. Glue longer pieces along the face and glue a few stray strands to the face, if desired.

13 Attach a silver chain with a charm.

4

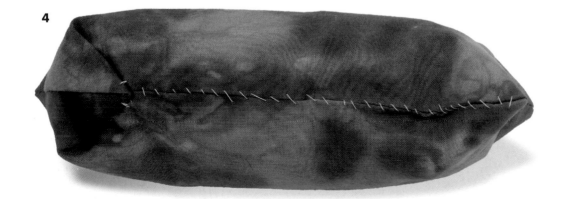

Art Doll with Clay Face II

This cloth art doll has only one arm showing which makes her a bit more abstract.

THE COMPLETE PHOTO GUIDE TO DOLL MAKING

YOU WILL NEED

- ½ yd. (0.46 m) printed cotton fabric
- fiberfill
- one clay face 2½" (6.4 cm) long
- one clay hand
- variegated brown crinkled ribbon yarn
- beads: 4 mm gold glass beads, gold seed beads, and triangular amber colored beads
- earrings: two gold headpins, four gold square beads, and two 14 mm gold glass beads
- necklace: metal charm and green hemp
- black beading thread
- beading needle
- basic sewing supplies
- round-nose pliers
- white craft glue
- hemostat
- weight bag

4 Stuff arm with fiberfill, using the hemostat.

5 Glue both sides of the bottom edge of the hand and push into the arm hole.

6 Attach the clay face to the head with beading thread through the three holes at the top of the head.

7 Make two hair pieces using ribbon yarn. Cut nine pieces 12" (30.5 cm) long. Lay one piece out flat and put the others over it. Tie.

8 Glue the knot of one hair piece at the center of the head with ribbons going down the back and the other knot at the top of the head, covering the holes and with the ribbons falling along the side of the face.

9 For earrings, glue a square gold bead on the gold headpin. Then put on the round glass bead and another square bead. With round-nosed pliers, bend the top of the headpin in a circle. Sew the earring on through the circle where an ear might be. When both earrings are in place, put a dot of glue on the circle and glue down one strand of hair to cover the circle.

10 Make a necklace from a length of hemp with a charm on it. Tie in back.

1 Trace the pattern on page 204 and cut it out. Fold fabric and cut two body pieces, using pattern as a guide. Cut one arm piece.

2 Follow steps 2 to 4 on page 157. Pin the arm piece on the body, with the long straight side along the side seam. Using a running stitch (page 180), attach arm to body, leaving the cuff edge open.

3 Outline the arm with the gold glass beads in two rows and the variegated beads in two rows down the side seam edge of the arm. These will cover the raw edges and the thread. Three rows of gold seed beads are placed along the cuff and then two rows of triangular beads are sewn along the cuff edge.

7

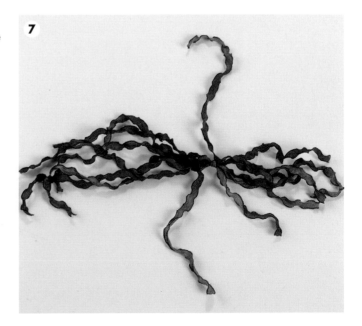

Cloth Dolls with Needle-Sculpted Faces

Meet Sarah and Ruth, cloth art dolls with needle-sculpted faces. Ruth was created to give a tangible figure to an image of the woman who gave up her old life to follow her husband and his family. Sara is very much like Ruth, but her wardrobe choices are very different. Needle sculpting allows the doll maker to create a three-dimensional face from fabrics. With needle and thread and some carefully placed stitches, the face begins to take shape and develop character. Practice on a sample doll face until you get the results you like.

Sarah

YOU WILL NEED

- scrap of muslin for Ruth's head and beige cotton scrap for head of Sarah

- off-white thread

- fiberfill

- colored pencils

- medium-tip and fine-tip black markers

- white paint

- variety of fibers for the hair (both dolls have some eyelash yarn in the hair bundle)

- glue

- hemostat

- basic sewing supplies

Ruth

Faces

1 Trace head pattern (page 200) onto the muslin or cotton and sew, using the sewing machine, on the shaped line. Do not sew the straight side. This is the top of the head. Cut out, leaving a ¼" (6 mm) seam allowance on all sides including the straight side.

2 Finger-press down the seam allowance at the straight side and turn.

3 Stuff the head with the fiberfill using the hemostat. Do not fill tightly. Make sure the nose bump is filled. Note: The machine stitch line is the center of the face. When sculpting the features on the face, the thread only goes to the outside at the back seam when knotting off.

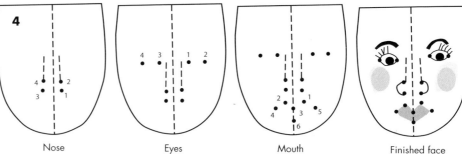

Nose   Eyes   Mouth   Finished face

4 Looking at the diagrams, begin sculpting the nose with the off-white thread. Secure thread at the back seam of the head and bring it through to the front and out at the right nostril (1).

(continued)

5 Make a small stitch and bring the needle up at the right inside curve of the nose (2).

6 Make a small stitch, pull, and come up at the left nostril (3). Make a small stitch, come up at the left curve of the nose (4). Pull. Repeat 1 through 4 once. Stitches will be on top of each other.

7 Starting at the curve in the nose, make three stitches up to the bridge of the nose, going from right to left inside the head with the seam line down the middle. Make sure to pull up fiberfill with the point of the needle before each stitch to fill nose up. Gently pull thread.

8 Bring needle out at the back seam and knot.

9 Eyes are made by making two small stitches each. The first stitch is across from the last stitch in the nose bridge and the second is about a ¼" (6 mm) across from the first. Repeat on the other side of the nose.

10 Bring the thread out at the back seam and knot.

11 The mouth is made up of six small stitches. The first two are directly below the nostril stitches (1 and 2). The next stitch is between these first stitches but lower and on the seam line (3). The last two stitches determine the width of the mouth and can vary from doll to doll (4 and 5); the last stitch is below the middle stitch on the seam line (6).

12 Bring the thread out at the back seam and knot.

13 Now add more fiberfill to the head and round out the cheeks. This addition can also even out any wrinkles in the face. Pack firmly.

14 With needle and thread, run a gathering stitch around the top of the head in the middle of the seam allowance. Pull tight and then stitch back and forth over the top to flatten.

Tip

Do not pull thread hard, as doing so will cause wrinkles.

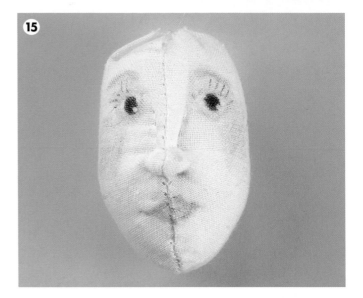

15 Color the face in with colored pencils. Dark brown is used to outline the eyes, eyebrows, and nose shadow. Lime green is used for eye shadow and shades of red for the lips and cheeks. Go lightly at first. The eye is made with the regular tip of the marker. Outline the eye, eyebrow, and add eyelashes with the fine tip. A final touch is the glint in the eye. This is done with a pin point dipped in white paint.

16 Make the hair pieces with desired yarns, following the method on page 159, step 7.

17 Glue hair to head. More than one bundle may be needed to cover.

YOU WILL NEED

- ¼ yd. (0.23 m) floral cotton fabric for Ruth and beige cotton fabric for Sarah
- fiberfill
- basic sewing supplies
- hemostat

Body

1 Copy the pattern pieces on page 200. Fold fabric right sides together and trace the pattern on the fabric. Make sure to trace two arms and two legs.

2 Stitch on the traced lines through both layers with the sewing machine. Do not stitch the straight lines. These are left open for stuffing.

3 Cut out, leaving a seam allowance on all sides including the straight side. Finger-press the allowance down on the straight side of each piece.

4 Turn all pieces using the hemostat. When turning the arms, first pull the thumb into the arm and then turn.

5 Push all seam allowances into the different pieces; then stuff with the fiberfill.

6 After body is well stuffed, slipstitch the bottom closed.

7 Stuff arms right up to the folded end; place at the side seam of the body, matching seams. Secure arm with two pins and stitch in place. Repeat for other arm. You will notice that one of Ruth's arms goes up and one down; Sarah's arms are both down. Remember thumbs are always up.

8 Attach the legs on the body in the same manner as the arms. Place the legs at the corners of the body with the seams facing front and back.

9 Sew the head to the neck, leaving the chin area free. The hair will cover this connection.

Bent Leg Variation

Lainie is made the same as the Ruth and Sarah except that she has bent legs. These legs are sewn to the bottom front of the body so that they stick straight out. Arms and legs can be bent by taking a few stitches on the inside of the elbow and knee joints. Pulling the stitches tightly makes the joints bend so that dolls can sit or carry things.

Sara's Dress

1 Turn under ½" (1.3 cm) hem on all sides; press and stitch on the machine ⅜" (1 cm) from the fold.

2 Draw up the triangle point opposite the longest side, between the doll's legs, from front to back. Stitch in place on back.

3 Pin long side of the triangle flat on the chest. Tack in place under the arms.

4 Wrap ends to the back and fold so the wrong side doesn't show. Parts of these folds will be visible in front to give a full look to the garment.

5 Slipstitch in place.

6 Stitch hands together around a stem of flowers.

YOU WILL NEED

• cotton print fabric triangle 10" x 10" x 15" (25.4 x 25.4 x 38.1 cm)

• basic sewing supplies

• small stem with flowers

5

6

YOU WILL NEED

- ¼ yd (0.23 m) printed cotton fabric

- two small buttons

- black and white paint

- small paintbrush

- thin silver chain and charm

- beading needle

- bird bead charm

- clear seed bead

- basic sewing supplies

Ruth

1 Paint boots on the feet, about 1½" (3.8 cm) tall.

2 When the black paint has dried, paint on white buttons using a pin. Dot the buttons up the center seam. Rewet the pin for each button to get buttons of the same size.

Tip

Prop the doll's legs up on a glue bottle or something to get both legs off of the work surface.

3 To make the coat, cut a piece of fabric 11" x 5" (27.9 x 12.7 cm).

4 With right sides together, sew ½" (1.3 cm) side seams to 1½" (3.8 cm) from the fold.

5 Find the center of one side and cut to within 1" (2.5 cm) of the fold. Then cut on the diagonal on each side to the fold. This is the front edge of the coat.

6 Turn inside out and press side seam flat. Press seam allowance flat around the arm hole openings. Press under ½" (1.3 cm) on each side up the front opening. Press down the V-shaped piece at the back of the neck and the V-shaped edges.

7 Fold up a ½" (1.3 cm) hem on the bottom and press flat.

8 Topstitch all hems about ⅜" (1 cm) from the fold.

9 Sew on the two button through both thicknesses.

10 Make a necklace by sewing one end of the thin chain to the back of the neck with the beading needle.

11 Add a charm to the chain.

12 Measure and cut the chain to length desired and stitch to the back of the neck.

13 Sew the bird to the upraised hand using the beading needle.

14 Secure thread in the hand and then place the bird and clear seed bead on the thread. Go back through the bird using the seed bead as the turn bead. Secure thread.

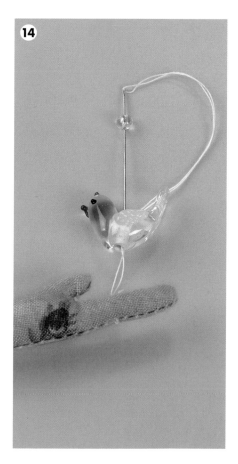

Cloth Doll with Encaustic Face

The face for this doll is drawn on fabric using wax crayons and then melted into the fabric using a hot plate. This encaustic technique is fun and you can get stunning results. Working in wax is also forgiving. If you make a mistake, it can easily be corrected or altered using white crayon.

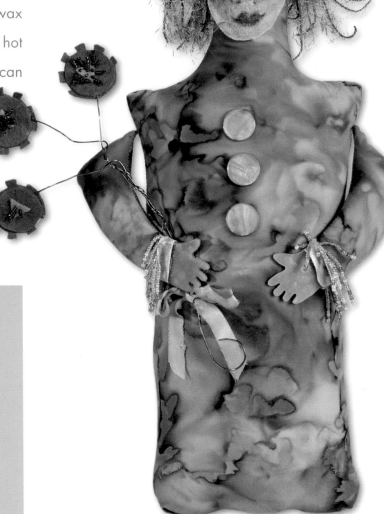

YOU WILL NEED

- hot plate
- fabric, dish towel weight
- crayons
- colored pencils
- polymer clay to make two clay hands
- ½ yd. (0.46 m) cotton print fabric
- eyelash yarn to go with the fabric
- fiberfill
- weight bag
- ½ yd. (0.46 m) beaded fringe and satin ribbon trim
- three ¾" (1.9 cm) flat round beads
- gold and purple felt scraps
- heavy copper wire
- purple seed beads
- beading thread and needle
- glue
- clip clothespins

1 Follow steps 1 to 6 for the encaustic face on page 112, but make the face on fabric instead of paper. Make clay hands, following the directions on page 155.

2 Trace the patterns on page 205. Cut two body pieces and four arm pieces. With right sides together, sew the doll body using a ⅜" (1 cm) seam. Leave an opening in the bottom. Turn right side out. Insert a weight bag into the bottom of the doll body to make it stand without tipping. Finish stuffing the doll with fiberfill. Slipstitch the opening closed.

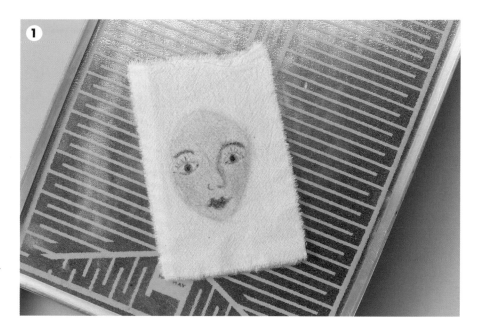

Tip

The weight bag can be made of marbles or rocks in a cloth or mesh bag.

3 With right sides together, stitch two arms leaving the cuff edge open. Turn right side out.

4 Apply glue to both sides of each wrist of the clay hands and push them into the cuff openings of the arms. Clip with a clothespin until dry.

5 Run a bead of glue around the wrist, covering the raw edge of the fabric. Wrap beaded trim around the wrist twice. Allow to dry.

6 Glue the face on the head of the doll.

7 Make two bundles of hair, using the yarn. Refer to page 159. Glue hair to head and trim. Glue a few wisps to the side of the face.

8 Glue the three flat beads, evenly spaced, down the front of the doll.

9 Measure down 1" (2.5 cm) from the shoulder and stitch the point of the arm at the side seam of the doll.

10 Lay the arms across the body of the doll and glue the hands in place. Insert long pins between the fingers of the hand to hold the hands to the body while drying.

11 To make flowers, cut three yellow triangles, each side ½" (1.3 cm). Cut purple circles as follows: three circles 1¼" (3.2 cm) in diameter, one circle 1⅜" (3.5 cm) in diameter, one circle 1½" (3.8 cm) in diameter, and one circle 1⅝" (4.1 cm) in diameter. Place a yellow triangle in the center of each small circle, and bead in place with the purple seed beads.

12 Glue one small circle onto one larger circle off center so both edges match in one place. Cut around the edge of the larger circle and remove every other piece to look like flower petals.

13 Cut three 12" (30.5 cm) pieces of copper wire for the flower stems. Slip one end of a piece of wire between the circles, where the edges match, for the stem. Clip with a clothespin to hold until dry. Glue the other two flowers and stems together.

14 When flowers are dry, twist the wire stems together and fan out the flowers. Put the stem under one hand as if the doll is holding the flowers. You may have to reglue the hand.

Art Doll Gallery

We have many dolls in our collections, some we have made and some given to us by friends. Each doll is unique, and they inspire us in different ways. Some are astonishingly complex or cleverly made. Their expressions or postures can evoke emotions or bring back memories.

Ascending into Myself by Rick Petersen. This is a self-portrait doll, made from polymer clay and fabric with wire armature body. Growing into or stepping into myself each day and becoming my potential, the envelopes have words and thoughts that are meaningful to my growth and learning to be creative.

Dauphine the Flower Girl by Rick Petersen. This cloth doll has button joints and a polymer clay face. The design is intended to give more lifelike features to flowers.

Elfona Box, by Rick Petersen, was created in response to a word challenge with an art group (whatever was made had to involve words). With simple elements—a metal container, polymer clay, and cloth—he formed this doll sitting on a container, like words that contain meaning: sometimes hidden, sometimes seen.

Keeper of the Solstice by Rick Petersen is made of cloth and polymer clay. He represents the summer and winter solstice with his face and the sun, and he is holding a face (the moon) that glows in the dark.

Squirrel Girl was made to commemorate an unusual meeting of a baby squirrel and the doll maker. The squirrel ran up my leg twice before he knew that I wasn't a tree. She holds a little book that tells about the encounter. Designed by Nancy Hoerner.

Latte da Coffee Doll Challenge by Rick Petersen. This doll, made of cloth, polymer clay, and coffee beans, was designed as part of an art doll exhibit for a coffee shop.

Mixed-Media Book Doll base created by Barbara Matthiessen. This doll was created in a round robin. The base was created then sent off to another artist who added to the doll and created a technique page for the book hidden inside the video box. This round robin lasted almost ten months with each artist having three weeks to complete their work then ship to the next artist in line.

Wood and Wire Dolls by Barbara Matthiessen. These dolls were inspired by Laurel Burch's designs combined with Native American and African patterns. The wood pieces were precut. Painting and detailing was done in layers to create a semi-random interesting pattern.

The Magician is a mixed-media doll created by Dorothy Egan and was presented to Barbara Matthiessen as a surprise gift. Art's Angels artist group created various pieces for each member's birthday. Barbara Matthiessen was presented with an array of amazing art dolls that represented some part of her nature or desires.

Life's a Journey, Barbara Matthiessen. Life's a Journey was created during a stressful time. The face is a blind self portrait done with markers. The limbs are a journal of random thoughts written with markers onto muslin. This could also be called a therapy doll.

Gloria the Doll Maker was made to honor a woman who makes dolls that look like they could talk. She was a great inspiration. The pattern for these dolls is the same as was used for Ruth (page 157) only the sizes differ.

Mixed-Media, created by Chris Malone, has bingo chip breasts. She was also a gift at the same celebration as The Magician (page 174). She has no name but lots of charm.

Green Beaded Doll by Nancy Hoerner, was created for a display showing not only a doll form but some bead work.

Embroidery Stitches

Use these stitches to embroidery doll faces or to embellish their clothes.

Straight Stitch

Bring the needle up to the right side of the fabric at your starting point. Insert the needle the desired distance from the starting point; then pull it to the back of the fabric.

Split Stitch

Make a small straight stitch. Then bring the needle to the right side again halfway along the stitch you've just made, splitting the thread with the tip of the needle. Repeat to the end of the line.

Backstitch

Bring the needle up to the right side of the fabric one stitch length from the starting point. Insert the needle at the starting point. Then bring it up again, two stitch lengths away. Pull the thread through, making a stitch. Repeat the first step, inserting your needle at the end of the stitch you just made.

Running Stitch

Bring the needle up to the right side of the fabric at your starting point. Push the needle in and out of the fabric along the pattern line, leaving a space between each stitch. Keep the stitches an even size and tension for a consistent look.

Chain Stitch

Bring the needle up to the right side of the fabric at your starting point. Hold the thread toward you with your free thumb, take a stitch into the same hole where the thread was brought up, forming a small loop. Bring the needle up through the fabric where you want the end of the stitch but do not pull the thread through yet. Bring the needle out and over the loop. Use your free hand to guide the thread around the needle making a second loop overlapping the first one. Repeat.

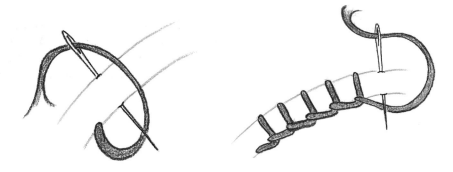

Blanket Stitch

Insert the needle from the right side of the fabric through to the back. Bring the needle up while holding the loop of thread with your left thumb. Make a vertical stitch, bringing the needle out over the loop made by the thread. Pull the needle through until the blanket stitch is snug against the fabric.

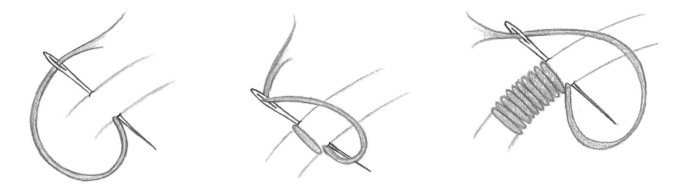

Satin Stitch

Bring the thread up to the right side of your fabric precisely on the pattern line. Insert the needle straight across the shape, on the opposite side. Bring the needle out again as close as possible to the end of the first stitch. Insert the needle into the fabric straight across the shape in the opposite direction to form the next satin stitch. Repeat to fill the shape.

French Knots

Bring the needle up through to the right side of the fabric. With your free hand, grip the thread about 2" (5 cm) from the spot and pull it taut but not tight. Wind the thread that is between your fingers and the fabric around the needle once. Continue holding the thread taut, while inserting the needle back into the starting point hole (or very close to it). Pull the thread through the wound loop and fabric to the wrong side. Secure the thread after each French knot. For larger knots, wind the thread around the needle two or three times.

Patterns

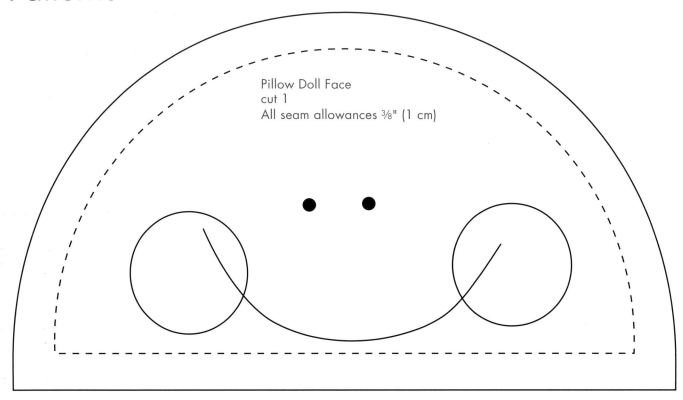

Pillow Doll Face
cut 1
All seam allowances ⅜" (1 cm)

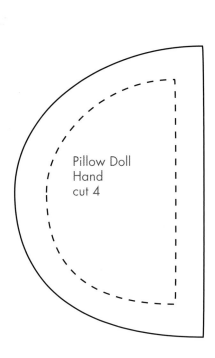

Pillow Doll
Hand
cut 4

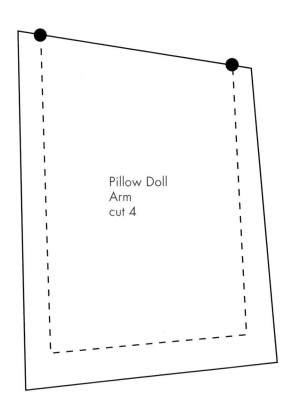

Pillow Doll
Arm
cut 4

Santa Sock Doll Mitten
cut 4

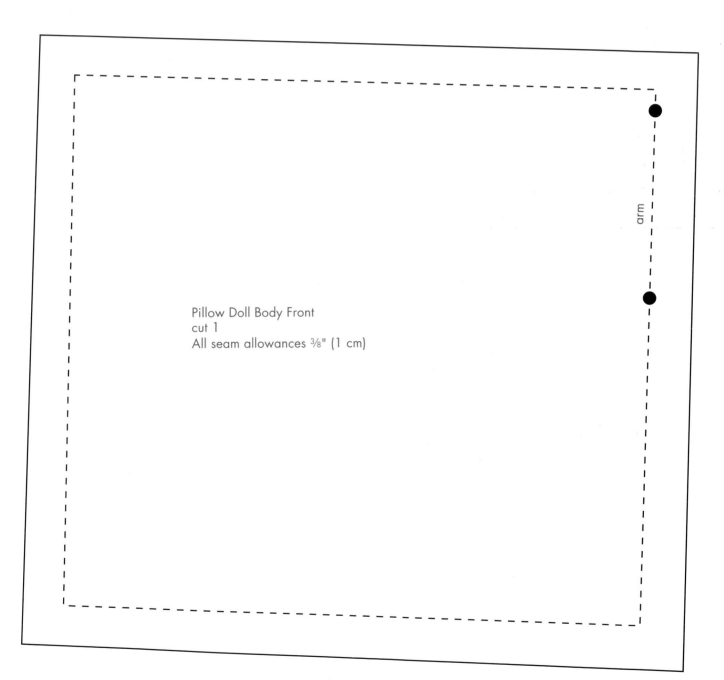

Pillow Doll Body Front
cut 1
All seam allowances ⅜" (1 cm)

arm

Pillow Doll Back
cut 1

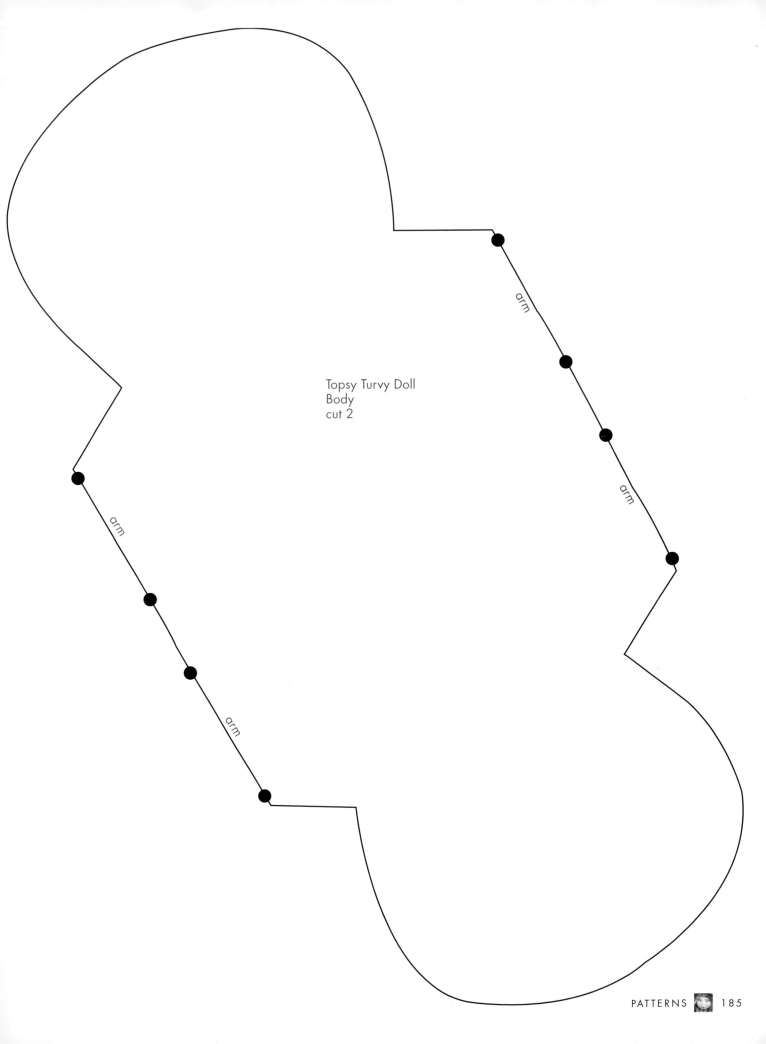

Topsy Turvy Doll
Body
cut 2

arm

arm

arm

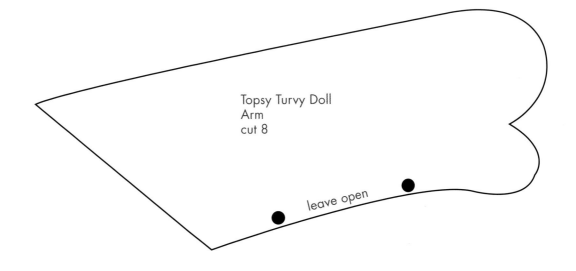

Topsy Turvy Doll
Arm
cut 8

leave open

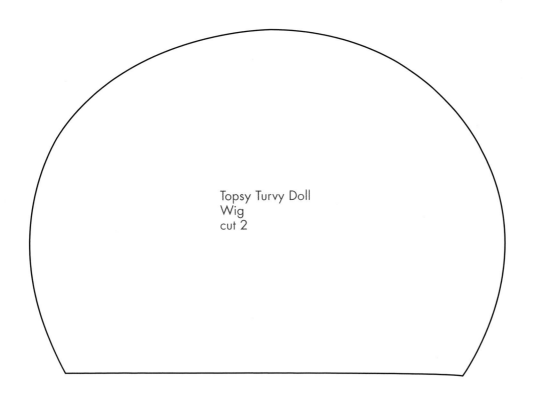

Topsy Turvy Doll
Wig
cut 2

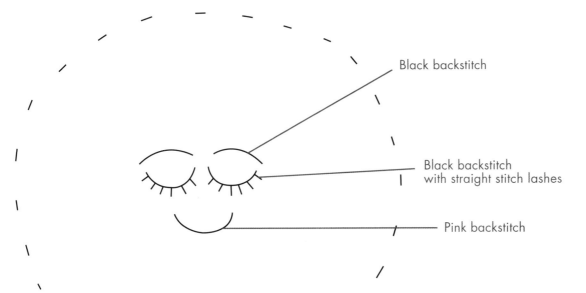

Black backstitch

Black backstitch
with straight stitch lashes

Pink backstitch

Topsy Turvy Faces

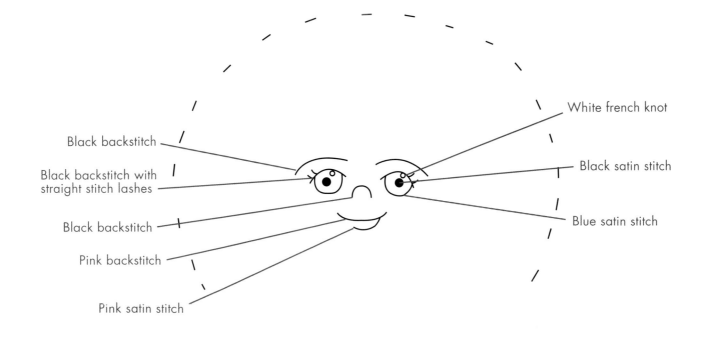

Black backstitch

Black backstitch with
straight stitch lashes

Black backstitch

Pink backstitch

Pink satin stitch

White french knot

Black satin stitch

Blue satin stitch

FOLD

Topsy Turvy Doll Dress and Nightgown
cut 1 dress on double fold
cut 1 nightgown on double fold

FOLD

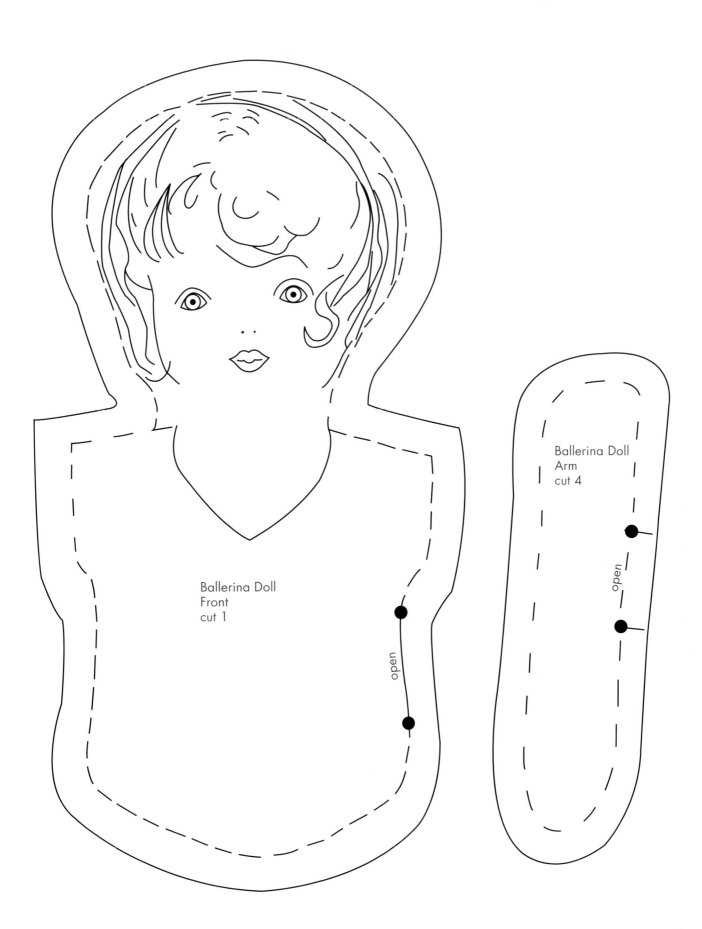

Ballerina Doll
Front
cut 1

open

Ballerina Doll
Arm
cut 4

open

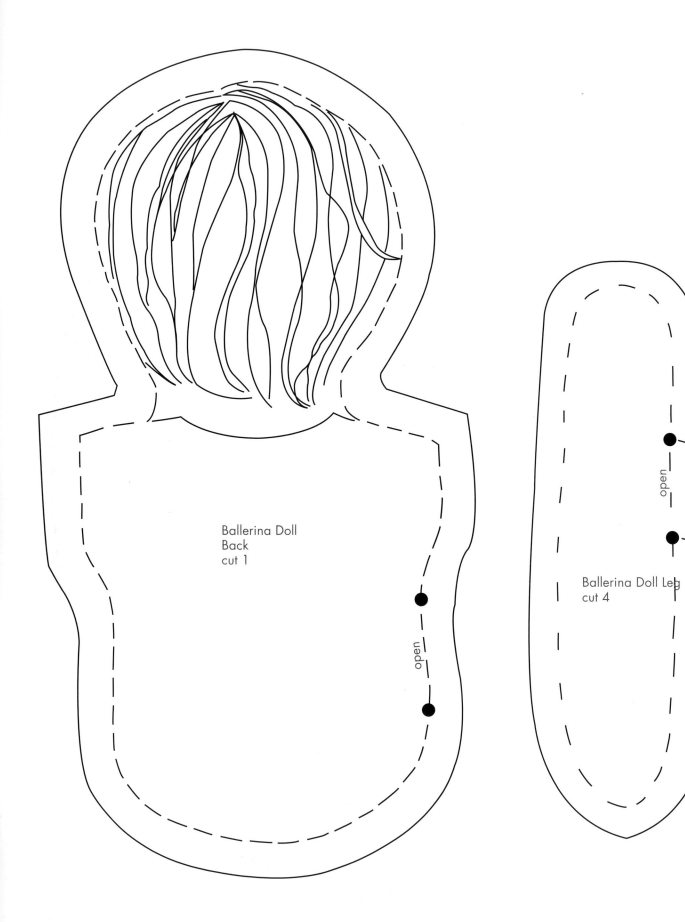

Ballerina Doll
Back
cut 1

open

Ballerina Doll Leg
cut 4

open

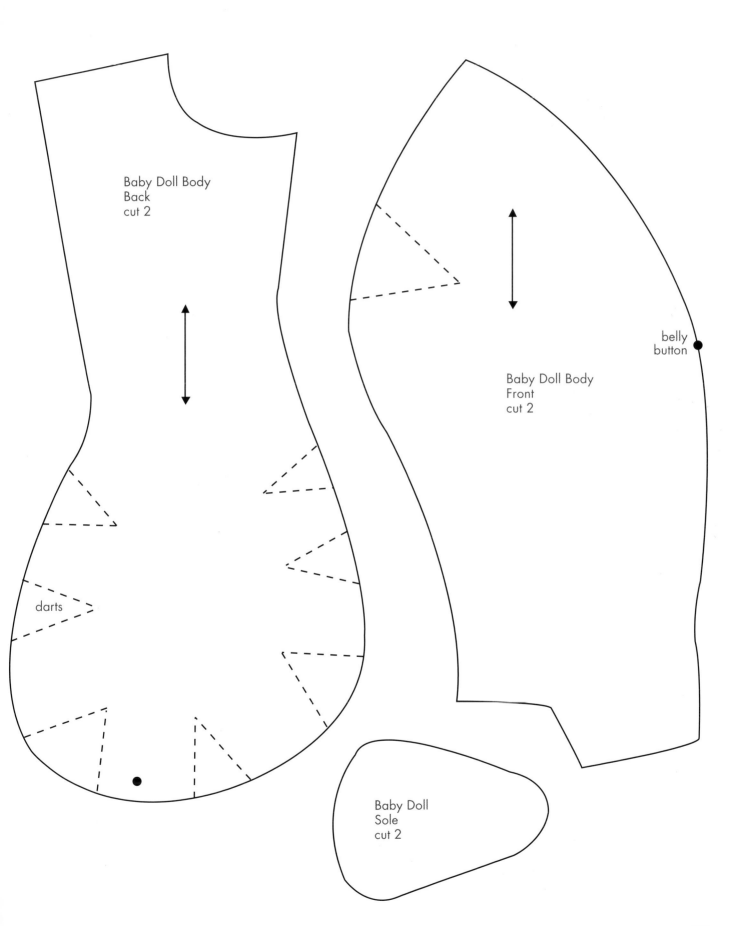

Baby Doll Body
Back
cut 2

darts

Baby Doll Body
Front
cut 2

belly
button

Baby Doll
Sole
cut 2

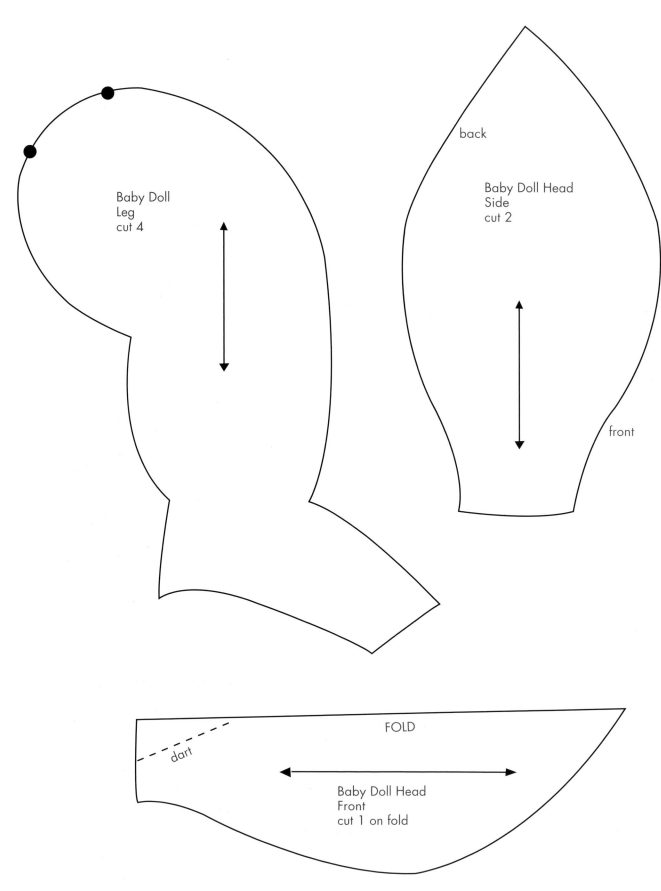

Baby Doll
Leg
cut 4

back

Baby Doll Head
Side
cut 2

front

FOLD

dart

Baby Doll Head
Front
cut 1 on fold

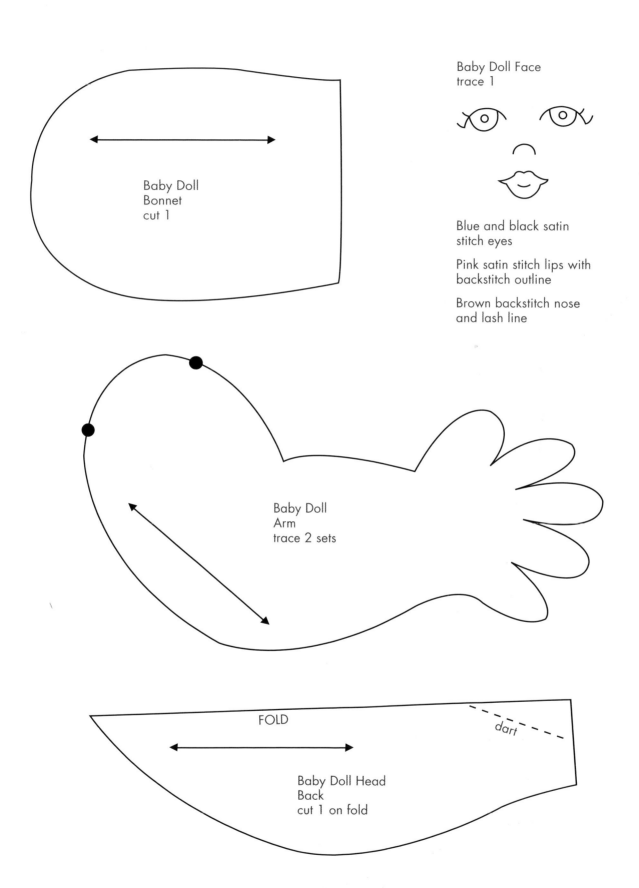

Baby Doll
Bonnet
cut 1

Baby Doll Face
trace 1

Blue and black satin
stitch eyes

Pink satin stitch lips with
backstitch outline

Brown backstitch nose
and lash line

Baby Doll
Arm
trace 2 sets

FOLD

dart

Baby Doll Head
Back
cut 1 on fold

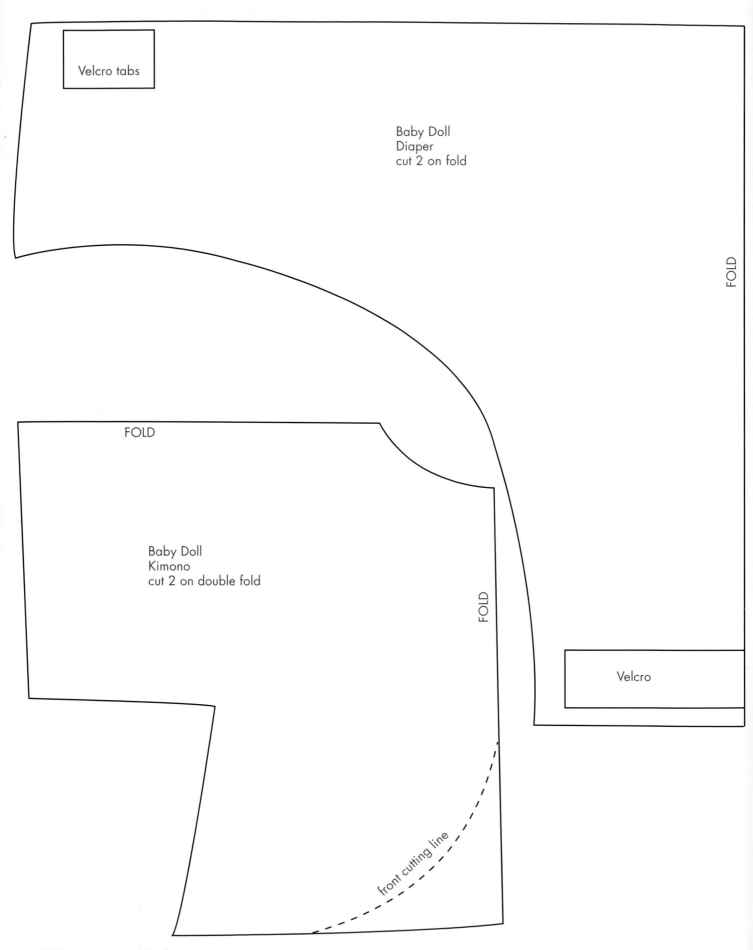

Velcro tabs

Baby Doll
Diaper
cut 2 on fold

FOLD

FOLD

Baby Doll
Kimono
cut 2 on double fold

FOLD

Velcro

front cutting line

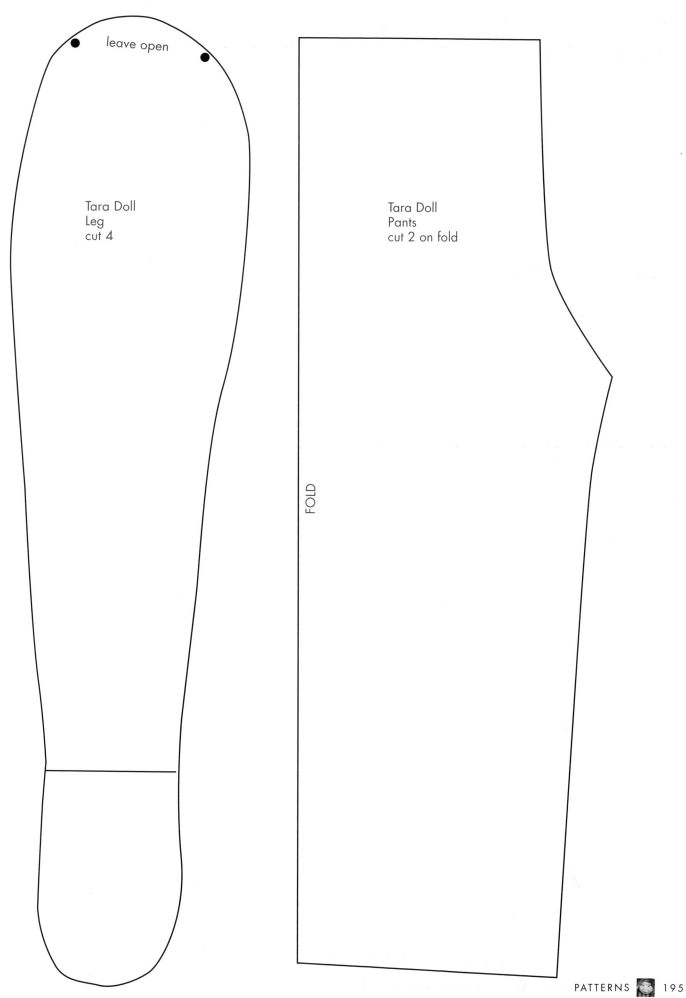

leave open

Tara Doll
Leg
cut 4

Tara Doll
Pants
cut 2 on fold

FOLD

FOLD

front neckline

cut for facing

Tara Doll
Tunic
cut 2 on fold

Tara Doll
Head/Face
cut 1

leave open

Tara Doll
Arm
cut 4

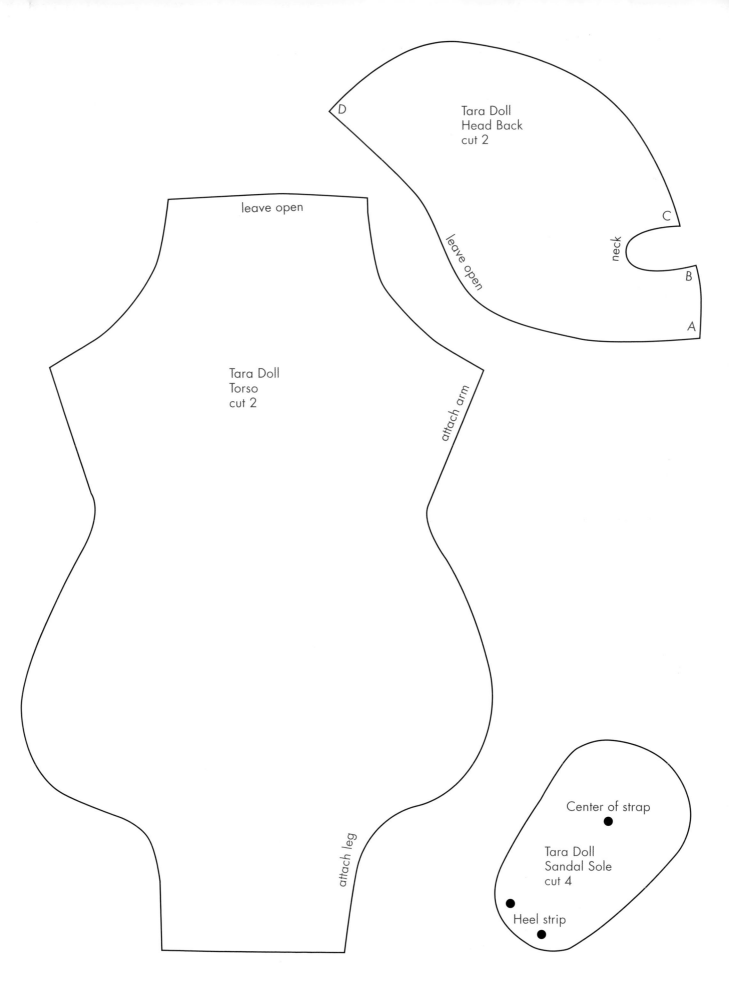

Tara Doll
Head Back
cut 2

D

leave open

C

neck

B

A

leave open

Tara Doll
Torso
cut 2

attach arm

attach leg

Center of strap

Tara Doll
Sandal Sole
cut 4

Heel strip

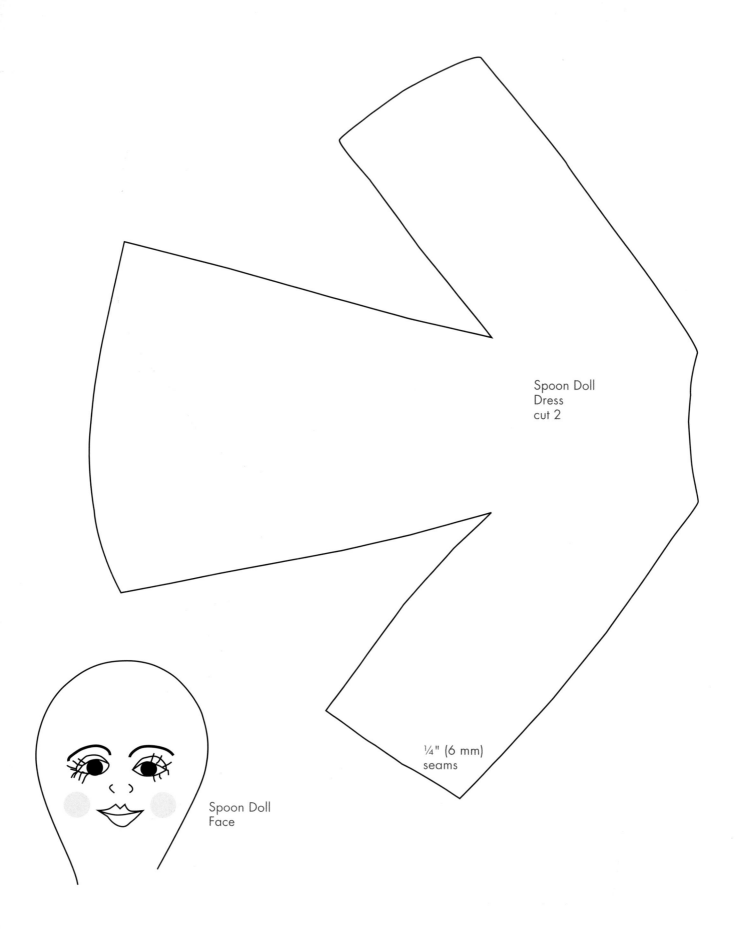

Spoon Doll
Dress
cut 2

¼" (6 mm)
seams

Spoon Doll
Face

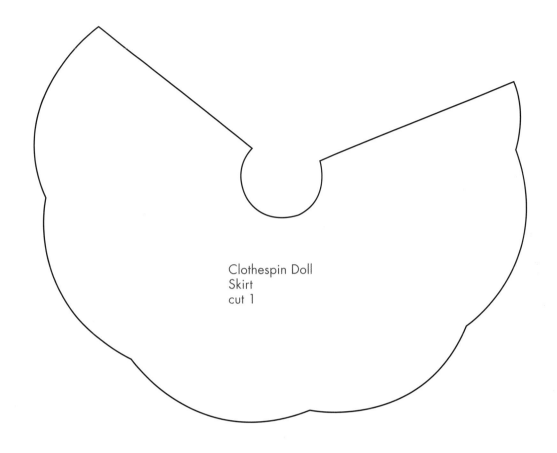

Clothespin Doll
Skirt
cut 1

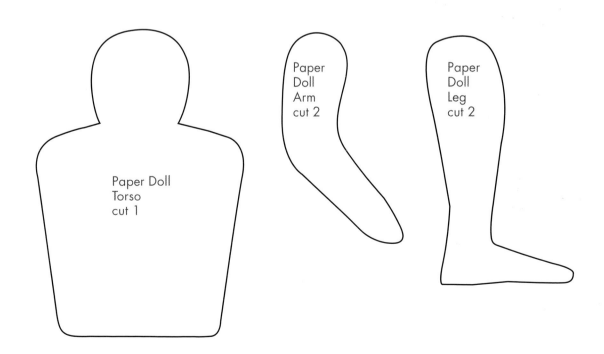

Paper Doll
Torso
cut 1

Paper
Doll
Arm
cut 2

Paper
Doll
Leg
cut 2

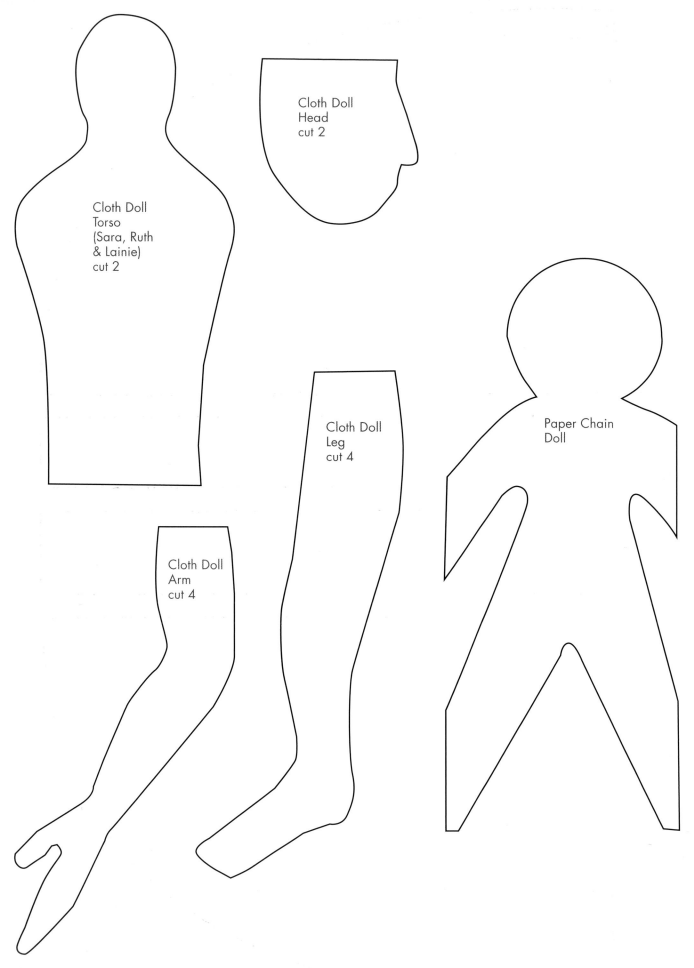

Cloth Doll
Head
cut 2

Cloth Doll
Torso
(Sara, Ruth
& Lainie)
cut 2

Cloth Doll
Leg
cut 4

Paper Chain
Doll

Cloth Doll
Arm
cut 4

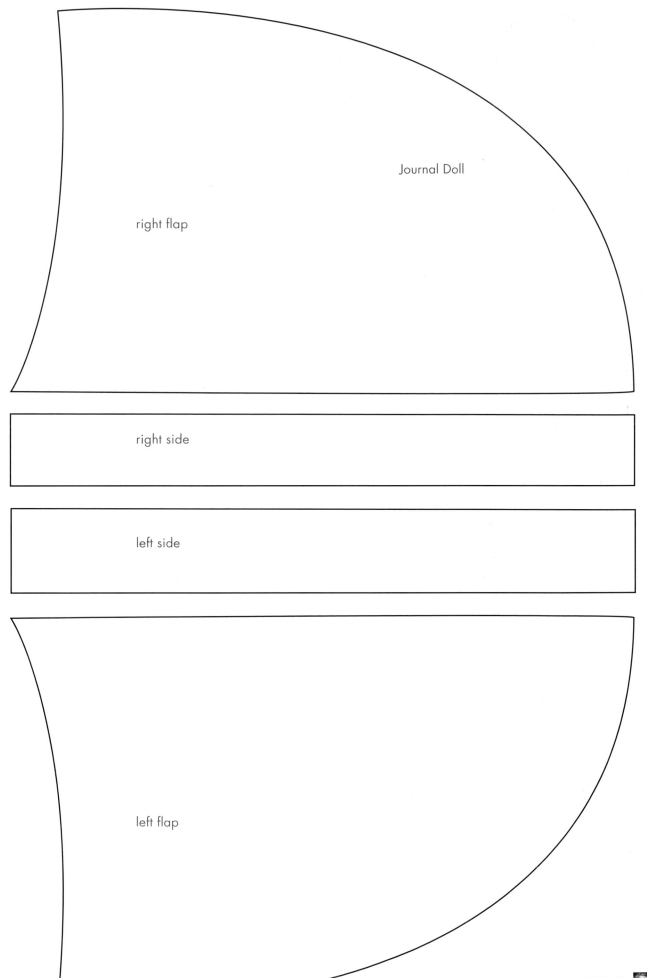

Journal Doll

right flap

right side

left side

left flap

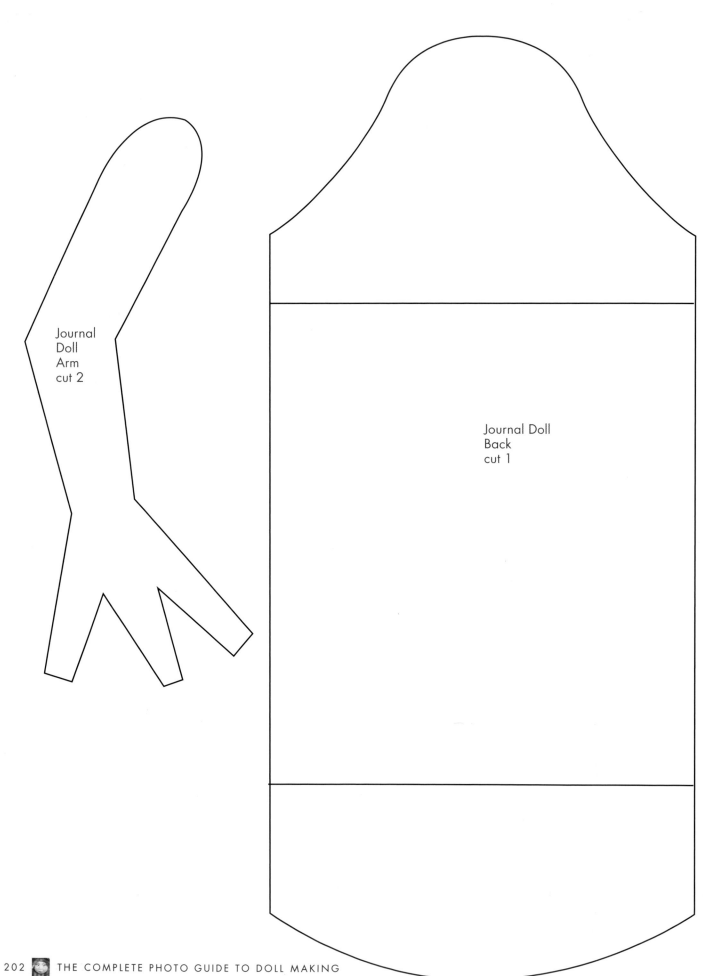

Journal
Doll
Arm
cut 2

Journal Doll
Back
cut 1

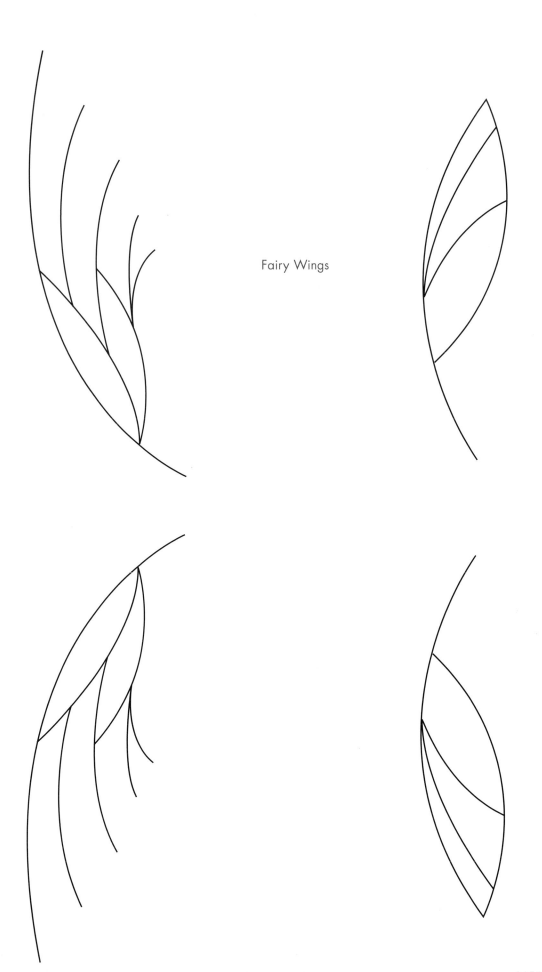

Fairy Wings

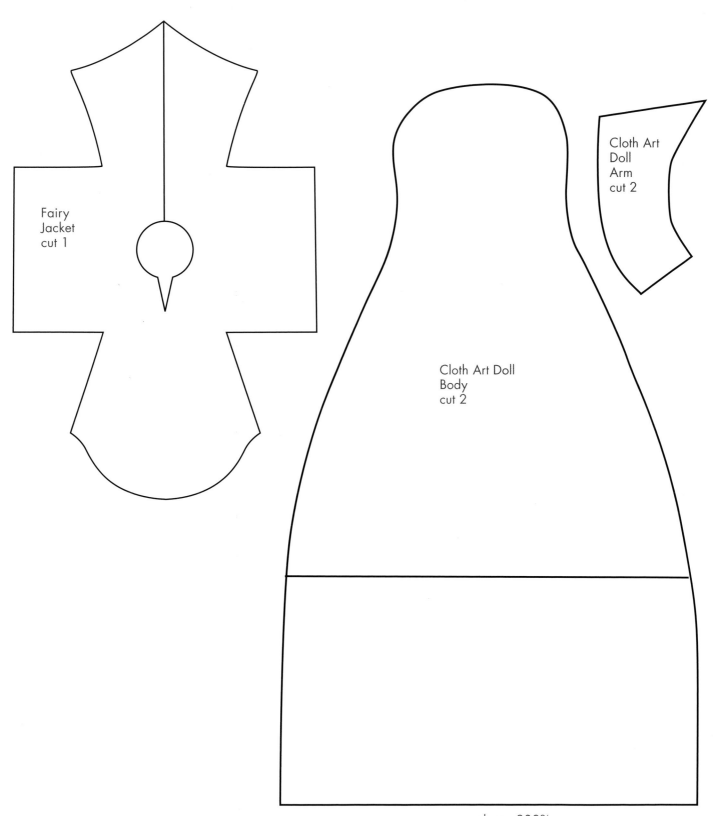

Fairy
Jacket
cut 1

Cloth Art Doll
Body
cut 2

Cloth Art
Doll
Arm
cut 2

enlarge 200%

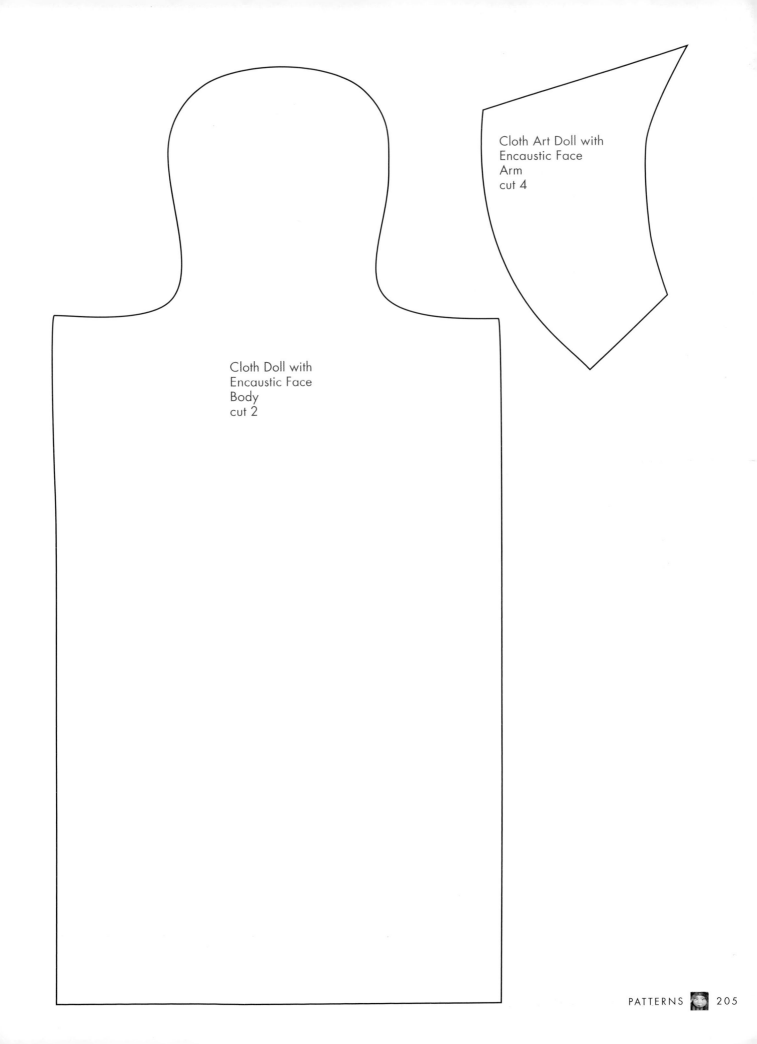

Cloth Art Doll with
Encaustic Face
Arm
cut 4

Cloth Doll with
Encaustic Face
Body
cut 2

Resources

Most of the supplies used for the projects in this book are readily available at fabric, quilt, craft, and art supply stores. Check these Internet sources for more information on how to use certain products or for retail stores that sell their products.

Clays:
www.polymerclayweb.com
www.katopolyclay.com
www.fimozone.com
www.sculpey.com
www.paperclay.com

Sources for specific products:
polymer clay push molds, including Moon Mold by Maureen Carlson
www.amaco.com

Bias cut ribbon
www.hanahsilk.com

Angelina fibers
www.texturatrading.com

Hand-shaped cookie cutters
www.amazon.com

Non toxic paints
www.earthsafe finishes.com

Doll and mixed media supplies
www.joggles.com

About the Authors

Nancy Hoerner

Combining fabric with an array of other mediums is Nancy's passion; she never finds enough hours in a day to try out all the fascinating possibilities. Nancy likes to work in layers, creating rich color and texture that is almost hypnotic with interest. Some of the mixed-media fabric pieces she creates stand alone and others are the base for further explorations.

Nancy's other interest is in the environment which is why she often replaces old supplies and techniques with cutting edge products used in unique ways.

Barbara Matthiessen

Barbara Matthiessen is a bestselling author and teacher. She has taught at numerous art retreats, developing many creative designs using innovative techniques which incorporate a wide range of crafts and materials. From her home in Port Orchard, Washington, she has worked for numerous manufacturers, creating multiple projects for sales models, trade show samples, and designs for magazines and project sheets. She has frequently been asked to work for manufacturers in their booths at trade shows. Her boundless energy and creative drive have inspired many people in the art world and other creative venues.

Barbara has served on the board and organized seminars for the Society of Craft Designers. She has also written monthly columns and/or served on the editorial board for several outstanding magazines. She is a frequent contributor to Belle Armoire and Somerset Studios Special Issue Publications such as Haute Handbags, Altered Couture, and Belle Armoire Jewelry.

Rick Petersen

As a child, Rick would entertain himself and friends for hours by drawing and creating things. Never one to follow the crowd, he was active in art at school and church, expressing myself through his art. He loved learning and making everything he could get his hands on. A few years ago Rick discovered polymer clay by taking a class from a local doll artist. This opened up a new way for him to express himself through what he creates. Art dolls soon become his focus and doll making is his creative outlet.

A graduate of Minneapolis College of Art and Design, Rick is the creative director of advertising for a local garden center. He lives in Edina, Minnesota with his wife, son, and daughter, and their two dogs, Henry and Emma.

Index

a

Ancestor photos, 91
Art Doll gallery, 168–178
Art Dolls with Clay Face I
    instructions, 156–157
    patterns, 204
Art Dolls with Clay Face II
    instructions, 158–159
    patterns, 204
Art Dolls with Encaustic Faces
    instructions, 166–167
    patterns, 205
Art Dolls with Needle-Sculpted Faces
    instructions, 160–165
    patterns, 200
Ascending into Myself Art Doll, 168

b

Baby Dolls (sock doll), 11–13
Baby Dolls, Woolen
    instructions, 38–46
    patterns, 191–194
Backstitch, explained, 179
Ballerina Dolls
    instructions, 34–37
    patterns, 189–190
Bark faces for nature dolls, 56–57
Batting, using, 126
Blanket stitch, explained, 180
Blind portraits, 91
Bone folders, using, 102
Book dolls
    Fabric Journal Dolls, 118–121, 201
    Flat Alice, 116–117
    Sunny Day Journals, 114–115
    techniques for making, 110–113
Brads, 99
Bubble wrap for paper dolls, 97

c

Cernit, about, 127
Chain of paper dolls
    instructions, 106–107
    pattern, 200
Chain stitch, explained, 180
Children, materials safe for, 9
Christmas Fairy dolls, 151
Christmas ornament, Soldier Clothespin, 77

Church dolls, 82–85
Clay. See Polymer clay
Clay dolls
    armatures, making, 124–126
    eyes and eyebrows, painting, 129, 131
    eyes, beaded, 146
    Garden Fairies, 140–151, 203–204
    mounting on base, 125
    removing fingerprints from, 147
    sculpted feet, making, 134–135
    sculpted hands, making, 132–133
    sculpted heads, making, 128–131
Clear fingernail polish print, 96
Cloth art dolls
    with Clay Face I, 156–157, 204
    with Clay Face II, 158–159, 204
    with Encaustic Faces, 166–167, 205
    faces, making, 154–155
    hands, making, 155
    with Needle-Sculpted Faces,
        160–165, 200
Clothespin Dolls
    instructions, 74–77
    pattern, 199
Copper wire, 124
Corn husk dolls, 62–63

d

Dauphine the Flower Girl Art Doll, 169

e

Elfona Box Art Doll, 169
Embossed toilet tissue for paper faces, 92
Embroidery stitches
    backstitch, explained, 179
    blanket stitch, explained, 180
    chain stitch, explained, 180
    French knot, explained, 181
    running stitch, explained, 180
    satin stitch, explained, 181
    split stitch, explained, 179
    straight stitch, explained, 179
Encaustic technique, explained, 94,
    112–113

f

Fabric Journal Dolls
    instructions, 118–121
    patterns, 201–202

Fairy Clothespin Dolls, 77
Family photos, 91
Felt Folk Angel Dolls, 47
Felt Modern-Style Dolls, 48–53
Fimo Classic, about, 127
Flat Alice (journal), 116–117
Folk Angel Dolls, 47
Folk dolls
    Clothespin Dolls, 74–77
    Felt Angel Dolls, 47
    Garden Glove Dolls, 86–87
    Hankie Dolls, 82–85
    Spool Dolls, 66–69
    Spoon Dolls, 70–73, 198
    Yarn Dolls, 78–81
French knots, explained, 181

g

Gallery of art dolls, 168–178
Garden Fairies
    instructions, 140–151
    patterns, 203–204
Garden Glove Dolls, 86–87
Gesso, using, 51
Gloria the Doll Maker Art Doll, 176
Green Beaded (Art) Doll, 178

h

Halloween Fairy dolls, 151
Hankie Dolls, 82–85
Hemostats, using, 41
Hollyhock dolls, 55
Hot plates, using, 112

i

Journal dolls
    Fabric Journal Dolls, 118–121,
        201–202
    Flat Alice, 116–117
    Sunny Day Journals, 114–115
    techniques for making, 110–113

k

Kato Polyclay, about, 127
Keeper of the Solistice Art Doll, 170

l

Lainie Art Dolls
    instructions, 160–165
    patterns, 200
Latte da Coffee Doll Challenge Art Doll, 172
Life's a Journey Art Doll, 175

m

The Magician Art Doll, 174
Materials safe for children, 9
Mixed-Media Art Doll, 177
Mixed-Media Book (Art) Doll, 172
Modern-Style Dolls, 48–53
Monster Dolls (sock doll), 21

n

Nature dolls
    corn husk dolls, 62–63
    hollyhock dolls, 55
    paper and stick dolls, 100–101
    rock and bark faces, 56–57
    Sarah Jane Pin Dolls, 58–59
    twig dolls, 60–61

p

Painting tip, 51
Pamphlet stitch, explained, 110–111
Paper and stick dolls, 100–101
Paper Chain Dolls
    instructions, 106–107
    pattern, 200
Paperclay and push molds, 93
Paper dolls
    bodies, making, 94–97
    chain of, making, 106–107, 200
    faces, making, 90–93
    movable, making, 98–99, 104–105
    patterns, 199
    tall, making, 102–103
Paper faces, making
    blind portrait, 91
    embossed toilet tissue, 92
    family photos, 91
    paperclay and push molds, 93
Paper towels, using, 117
Peltex and WonderUnder, 119
Pew dolls, 82–85
Pillow Dolls
    instructions, 22–25
    patterns, 182–184

Plants for twig dolls, 61
Plastic wrap for paper dolls, 97
Polymer clay
    about, 127
    cloth art doll faces, making, 154–155
    cloth art doll hands, making, 155
    eyes and eyebrows, painting, 129, 131
    eyes, beaded, 146
    Garden Fairies, 140–151, 203–204
    removing fingerprints from, 147
    sculpted feet, making, 134–135
    sculpted hands, making, 132–133
    sculpted heads, making, 128–131
Premo, about, 127
Punch, Judy and Lulu puppets, 104–105
Push mold faces, 93, 136–137

r

Rock faces for nature dolls, 56–57
Running stitch, explained, 180
Ruth Art Dolls
    instructions, 160–165
    patterns, 200

s

Safety factors, 9
Santa Dolls (sock doll)
    instructions, 14–20
    mitten pattern, 183
Sarah Art Dolls
    instructions, 160–165
    patterns, 200
Sarah Jane Pin Dolls, 58–59
Satin stitch, explained, 181
Sculpey, about, 127
Sock dolls
    Baby Dolls, 11–13
    Monster Dolls, 21
    Santa Dolls, 14–20, 183
    supplies, 10
Soft dolls
    Art Dolls with Needle-Sculpted Faces, 160–165
    Baby Dolls, 11–13
    Ballerina Dolls, 34–37, 189–190
    with Encaustic Faces, 166–167
    Garden Glove Dolls, 86–87
    Hankie Dolls, 82–85
    Monster Dolls, 21
    Pillow Dolls, 22–25, 182–184
    Santa Dolls, 14–20, 183
    Tara Dolls, 48–53, 195–197
    Topsy Turvy Dolls, 26–33, 185–188

    Woolen Baby Dolls, 38–46
    Yarn Dolls, 78–81
Soldier Clothespin Dolls, 77
Split stitch, explained, 179
Spool Dolls, 66–69
Spoon Dolls
    instructions, 70–73
    patterns, 198
Squirrel Girl Art Doll, 171
Stick and paper dolls, 100–101
Straight stitch, explained, 179
Sunny Day Journals, 114–115

t

Tall paper dolls, making, 102–103
Tara Dolls
    instructions, 48–53
    patterns, 195–197
Topsy Turvy Dolls
    instructions, 26–33
    patterns, 185–188
Tweaked push mold faces, 136–139
Twig and paper dolls, 100–101
Twig dolls, 60–61

w

Wax paper for paper dolls, 95
WonderUnder and Peltex, 119
Wood and Wire (Art) Dolls, 173
Woolen Baby Dolls, 38–46
Wool felt Folk Angel Dolls, 47
Wool felt Modern-Style Dolls, 48–53

y

Yarn Dolls, 78–81